THIS BOOK

BELONG   TO

....

....

Thank you for Purchasing my book and taking the time to read it from front to back. I am always grateful when a reader chooses my work and I hope you enjoyed it!

With the vast selection available online, I am touched that you chose to be purchasing my work and take valuable time out of your life to read it. My hope is that you feel you made the right decision.

I very much would like to know what you thought of the book. Please take the time to write an honest and informative review on Amazon.com. Your experience and opinions will be of great benefit to me and those readers looking to make an informed choice.

With much thanks.

Table of Contents

SUMMARY

What is Macramé?: Macramé is a form of textile art that involves creating intricate patterns and designs by knotting cords or threads together. It is believed to have originated in the 13th century in the Arab world and later spread to Europe during the Moorish conquests. The word "macramé" is derived from the Arabic word "migramah," which means "fringe."

Traditionally, macramé was used to create decorative and functional items such as wall hangings, plant hangers, and clothing accessories. It gained popularity during the Victorian era when it was used to adorn homes and clothing. However, it experienced a resurgence in the 1970s as a popular craft form associated with the hippie and bohemian movements.

Macramé involves using various types of knots to create intricate patterns and designs. The most commonly used knots in macramé include the square knot, half hitch knot, and double half hitch knot. These knots are repeated and combined in different ways to create unique and visually appealing designs.

One of the key features of macramé is its versatility. It can be done using a wide range of materials, including cotton, hemp, jute, and nylon. The choice of material can greatly impact the final look and feel of the macramé piece. For example, using a thick and sturdy material like jute can create a more rustic and bohemian look, while using a soft and delicate material like cotton can create a more delicate and feminine look.

Macramé can be done using various techniques, including knotting, weaving, and braiding. Each technique offers different possibilities for creating different textures and patterns. For example, knotting involves tying knots in a specific sequence to create patterns, while weaving involves intertwining cords to create a woven effect.

In recent years, macramé has gained popularity as a form of DIY craft and has become a trendy home decor choice. It is often used to create unique and personalized pieces such as wall hangings, curtains, and plant hangers. Macramé workshops and tutorials are also widely available, allowing people to learn and practice this ancient craft form.

Overall, macramé is a versatile and creative form of textile art that allows individuals to express their creativity and create beautiful and intricate designs. Whether used for functional or decorative purposes, macramé adds a unique and handmade touch to any space.

The Charm and Versatility of Knotting in Macramé: Macramé, an ancient art form that involves knotting cords to create intricate patterns, has been gaining popularity in recent years. The charm and versatility of this technique have captivated crafters and artists alike, leading to a resurgence in its practice and exploration.

One of the most appealing aspects of macramé is its simplicity. With just a few basic knots, such as the square knot and the half hitch, one can create stunning designs. This accessibility makes it an ideal craft for beginners, as well as a satisfying and relaxing activity for experienced artisans. The repetitive nature of knotting in macramé can be meditative, allowing practitioners to find a sense of calm and focus while creating something beautiful.

Furthermore, macramé offers a wide range of possibilities for creativity and self-expression. The versatility of this technique allows for the incorporation of various materials, such as different types of cords, beads, and even natural elements like driftwood or feathers. This flexibility enables artists to experiment with different textures, colors, and patterns, resulting in unique and personalized pieces.

Macramé can be used to create a variety of items, from small accessories like bracelets and keychains to larger home decor pieces like wall hangings and plant hangers. The ability to customize the size and design of these creations makes macramé a versatile craft that can be adapted to suit any space or personal style.

In addition to its aesthetic appeal, macramé also offers practical benefits. The durability of the knots used in this technique ensures that the finished pieces are sturdy and long-lasting. This makes macramé an excellent choice for creating functional items like bags or hammocks, as well as decorative pieces that can withstand the test of time.

Moreover, macramé provides a sense of connection to the past. This art form has been practiced for centuries, with its origins dating back to ancient civilizations. By engaging in macramé, modern crafters can tap into this rich history and carry on a tradition that has been passed down through generations.

Overall, the charm and versatility of knotting in macramé make it a captivating and rewarding craft. Whether you are a beginner looking for a new hobby or an experienced artist seeking a creative outlet, macramé offers endless possibilities for self-expression and exploration. Its simplicity, versatility, and practicality make it a craft that can be enjoyed by people of all ages and skill levels. So why not give macramé a try and discover the joy of knotting?

History and Resurgence of Macramé: Macramé, a form of textile art that involves knotting rather than weaving or knitting, has a rich and fascinating history that spans centuries. The word "macramé" is derived from the Arabic word "miqramah," which means "fringe." This art form has been practiced by various cultures around the world, including the ancient Egyptians, Persians, and Arabs.

The origins of macramé can be traced back to the 13th century when Arabian weavers began using intricate knotting techniques to create decorative fringes on their textiles. These fringes were not only aesthetically pleasing but also served functional purposes, such as preventing the edges of the fabric from unraveling. The art of macramé then spread to Europe through trade routes, where it gained popularity during the Renaissance period.

During the 17th and 18th centuries, macramé became particularly fashionable in England and France. It was used to create elaborate lace-like patterns that adorned clothing, curtains, and household items. Macramé was considered a highly skilled craft, and its intricate designs were often reserved for the wealthy and aristocratic.

However, with the advent of industrialization in the 19th century, macramé fell out of favor as mass-produced textiles became more readily available. The art form was largely forgotten until the mid-20th century when it experienced a resurgence in popularity.

In the 1960s and 1970s, macramé experienced a revival as part of the larger hippie and bohemian movements. The counterculture of the time embraced macramé as a way to express individuality and creativity. Macramé plant hangers, wall hangings, and jewelry became iconic symbols of the era.

Today, macramé continues to be a popular craft form, with artists and enthusiasts exploring new techniques and pushing the boundaries of traditional designs. The internet and social media platforms have played a significant role in the resurgence of macramé, allowing artists to share their work and inspire others around the world.

Contemporary macramé artists often incorporate modern materials and styles into their creations, blending traditional knotting techniques with a contemporary aesthetic. Macramé workshops and classes have also become increasingly popular, providing individuals with the opportunity to learn and practice this ancient art form.

In conclusion, the history and resurgence of macramé highlight its enduring appeal and versatility as a textile art form.

Various Applications in Modern Décor of Macramé: Macramé, a textile art form that involves knotting cords together to create intricate patterns and designs, has seen a resurgence in popularity in recent years. This ancient craft has found its way into various applications in modern décor, adding a touch of bohemian elegance and a sense of handmade artistry to any space.

One of the most common uses of macramé in modern décor is in the form of wall hangings. These large-scale pieces can serve as a focal point in a room, adding texture and visual interest to bare walls. Macramé wall hangings come in a variety of styles, from simple geometric patterns to more intricate designs featuring feathers, beads, and other embellishments. They can be hung alone or grouped together to create a gallery wall effect.

Another popular application of macramé in modern décor is in the form of plant hangers. These hanging plant holders not only provide a stylish way to display your favorite greenery but also add a touch of natural beauty to any room. Macramé plant hangers come in various lengths and designs, allowing you to create a customized display that suits your space and personal style. Whether you prefer a minimalist look with a single plant or a more bohemian vibe with multiple hanging plants, macramé plant hangers offer endless possibilities.

In addition to wall hangings and plant hangers, macramé can also be incorporated into other decorative elements in modern décor. For example, macramé curtains can add a soft and romantic touch to windows, allowing light to filter through the intricate patterns. Macramé table runners and placemats can elevate the look of a dining table, adding texture and visual interest to the setting. Macramé lampshades can create a warm and cozy ambiance, casting beautiful patterns of light and shadow in a room.

Furthermore, macramé can be used to create functional items in modern décor. Macramé baskets and storage containers offer a stylish way to organize and declutter your space, while macramé room dividers can create a sense of privacy and separation in open-concept living areas. Macramé pillows and throws can add a cozy and tactile element to sofas and beds, inviting you to snuggle up and relax.

Overall, the various applications of macramé in modern décor allow for endless creativity and personalization. Whether you choose to incorporate macramé as a statement piece or as subtle accents, this versatile craft adds a unique and handmade touch to any space,…

Understanding Materials and Tools of Macramé: Macramé is a popular craft that involves creating intricate patterns and designs using various materials and tools. In order to fully understand and master the art of macramé, it is important to have a comprehensive knowledge of the materials and tools that are commonly used in this craft.

One of the most essential materials in macramé is the cord. The cord is what forms the base of the macramé project and is used to create the knots and patterns. There are various types of cords that can be used in macramé, including cotton, nylon, jute, and hemp. Each type of cord has its own unique characteristics and properties, which can affect the overall look and feel of the finished project. For example, cotton cords are soft and pliable, making them ideal for creating delicate and intricate designs, while nylon cords are more durable and can withstand heavier weights, making them suitable for creating larger and sturdier macramé pieces.

In addition to cords, other materials commonly used in macramé include beads, charms, and pendants. These decorative elements can be incorporated into the macramé design to add visual interest and personalization. Beads can be threaded onto the cords and used as accents within the knots, while charms and pendants can be attached to the finished macramé piece to create a focal point or highlight a specific design element.

When it comes to tools, there are a few key items that every macramé artist should have in their toolkit. One of the most important tools is a pair of scissors. Scissors are used to cut the cords to the desired length and to trim any excess material. It is important to have a sharp pair of scissors that can easily cut through the cords without fraying or damaging them.

Another essential tool is a macramé board or a clipboard. This tool is used to hold the cords in place while working on the macramé project. It provides a stable surface for creating the knots and patterns, ensuring that the cords stay in place and do not become tangled or twisted.

In addition to these basic tools, there are also specialized tools that can be used to enhance and refine the macramé process. One such tool is a macramé comb or brush. This tool is used to comb through the cords and create a smooth and uniform appearance. It can be particularly useful when working with thicker cords or when creating intricate designs that require precise placement of the knots.

An Illustrated Guide to Basic Knots of Macramé: An Illustrated Guide to Basic Knots of Macramé is a comprehensive and visually appealing resource that aims to equip beginners with the necessary knowledge and skills to master the art of macramé. This guide goes beyond just providing a list of basic knots; it delves into the intricacies of each knot, offering step-by-step instructions accompanied by detailed illustrations.

The guide begins by introducing the reader to the history and origins of macramé, providing a fascinating background that helps to contextualize the importance and relevance of the knots being taught. It then proceeds to explain the essential tools and materials required for macramé, ensuring that readers are well-prepared before embarking on their creative journey.

The heart of this guide lies in its comprehensive coverage of the basic knots used in macramé. Each knot is meticulously explained, with clear instructions on how to create it and how it can be incorporated into various macramé projects. The illustrations accompanying each step are not only visually appealing but also serve as a valuable visual aid, making it easier for beginners to grasp the techniques involved.

Furthermore, this guide goes beyond just teaching the knots themselves; it also provides practical tips and tricks to help readers troubleshoot common mistakes and challenges that may arise during the knotting process. This ensures that beginners are not only equipped with the technical knowledge but also the problem-solving skills necessary to overcome any hurdles they may encounter.

In addition to the step-by-step instructions, this guide also includes inspiring project ideas that showcase the versatility of macramé and how the basic knots can be combined to create stunning and unique pieces. From wall hangings to plant hangers, readers will find a plethora of creative ideas that will ignite their imagination and encourage them to explore their own artistic expression.

What sets this guide apart from others is its attention to detail and its user-friendly approach. The explanations are clear and concise, making it accessible to beginners with no prior experience in macramé. The illustrations are not only aesthetically pleasing but also serve as a valuable visual aid, ensuring that readers can easily follow along and replicate the knots accurately.

Overall, An Illustrated Guide to Basic Knots of Macramé is an invaluable resource for anyone interested in learning the art of macramé. Whether you are a complete novice or have some experience, this guide will equip you with the necessary skills and knowledge to create beautiful macramé pieces.

Combining Knots for Textures and Patterns of Macramé: Combining Knots for Textures and Patterns of Macramé is a comprehensive guide that explores the art of macramé and provides detailed instructions on how to create various textures and patterns using different types of knots.

Macramé is a versatile craft that involves creating intricate designs by tying knots in various patterns. This book delves into the different types of knots that can be used in macramé and demonstrates how they can be combined to create stunning textures and patterns.

The book begins with an introduction to the history and origins of macramé, providing readers with a deeper understanding of the craft. It then moves on to explain the basic techniques and materials needed to get started, ensuring that even beginners can follow along and create beautiful macramé pieces.

One of the highlights of this book is its extensive collection of knot patterns. Each pattern is accompanied by step-by-step instructions and detailed illustrations, making it easy for readers to replicate the designs. From simple knots like the square knot and the half hitch knot to more complex knots like the double half hitch knot and the Josephine knot, this book covers a wide range of knotting techniques.

In addition to knot patterns, this book also explores how different combinations of knots can be used to create unique textures and patterns. It provides examples of various macramé projects, such as wall hangings, plant hangers, and jewelry, showcasing how different knot combinations can be used to achieve different effects.

Furthermore, the book offers tips and tricks for troubleshooting common macramé problems, such as loose knots or uneven tension. It also provides guidance on selecting the right materials and tools for each project, ensuring that readers have all the information they need to create successful macramé pieces.

Whether you are a beginner looking to learn the basics of macramé or an experienced macramé artist looking to expand your repertoire, Combining Knots for Textures and Patterns of Macramé is a valuable resource. Its detailed instructions, extensive knot patterns, and inspiring project ideas make it a must-have for anyone interested in the art of macramé.

Practice Projects: Simple Bracelets and Keychains of Macramé: In this practice project, we will be exploring the art of macramé by creating simple bracelets and keychains. Macramé is a technique that involves knotting cords together to create decorative and functional items. It is a versatile craft that allows for endless creativity and customization.

To begin, gather your materials. You will need a selection of cords in various colors, scissors, and any additional embellishments you may want to add, such as beads or charms. The cords can be made of different materials, such as cotton, nylon, or hemp, depending on your preference.

Start by cutting your cords to the desired length. For bracelets, a typical length is around 12 inches, while keychains can be longer, around 18 inches. You can adjust the length based on your personal preference and the size of the wrist or keychain you are making.

Next, choose the type of knot you want to use for your project. There are several basic knots in macramé, including the square knot, the half hitch knot, and the spiral knot. Each knot creates a different pattern and texture, so feel free to experiment and try different combinations.

Once you have chosen your knot, begin by securing the cords together at one end. This can be done by tying a simple knot or using a clip or safety pin to hold them in place. Then, start knotting the cords together, following the pattern you have chosen. You can alternate colors, create stripes, or even incorporate beads or charms into your design.

As you continue knotting, you will see your bracelet or keychain taking shape. Take your time and make sure each knot is tight and secure. If you make a mistake, don't worry! Macramé is forgiving, and you can easily undo knots and start again.

Once you have reached the desired length for your bracelet or keychain, finish off the ends by tying a secure knot. You can also add additional embellishments, such as beads or charms, by threading them onto the cords before tying the final knot.

Finally, trim any excess cord and tidy up the ends. You can leave them as they are for a more rustic look or use a lighter to carefully melt the ends to prevent fraying.

Congratulations! You have successfully created a simple macramé bracelet or keychain. These projects are great for beginners and provide a foundation for more complex macramé designs. With practice, you can explore more intricate patterns and techniques to create stunning macramé pieces

Designing Macramé Bracelets and Necklaces of Macramé:

A Creative Journey into the World of Macramé

Macramé, an ancient art form that involves knotting cords to create intricate patterns, has been gaining popularity in recent years. With its versatility and endless design possibilities, macramé has become a favorite among craft enthusiasts and fashion-forward individuals. In this article, we will delve into the art of designing macramé bracelets and necklaces, exploring the techniques, materials, and inspiration behind these stunning accessories.

To begin our creative journey, let's first understand the basics of macramé. The technique primarily involves using various knots to create patterns and textures. The most commonly used knots in macramé include the square knot, half hitch knot, and the lark's head knot. By combining these knots and experimenting with different cord colors and thicknesses, one can create unique and visually appealing designs.

When it comes to materials, macramé offers a wide range of options. Traditionally, natural fibers such as cotton, hemp, and jute were used. However, modern macramé artists have expanded their horizons by incorporating synthetic fibers like nylon and polyester, as well as metallic threads and even beads. These materials not only add a touch of glamour but also enhance the overall durability and longevity of the finished piece.

Now, let's dive into the design process. The first step is to decide on the style and theme of your macramé bracelet or necklace. Are you aiming for a bohemian, beachy vibe or a more elegant and sophisticated look? Once you have a clear vision in mind, you can start sketching out your design or create a mood board for inspiration. Pinterest and Instagram are great platforms to explore various macramé designs and gather ideas.

Next, it's time to choose the right cords for your project. Consider the thickness, color, and texture of the cords, as they will greatly influence the final outcome. Thicker cords are ideal for chunkier designs, while thinner cords work well for delicate and intricate patterns. Experimenting with different colors and textures can add depth and visual interest to your piece.

Once you have your cords ready, it's time to start knotting. Begin by securing the cords to a sturdy surface or a macramé board. This will provide stability and make the knotting process easier.

Incorporating Beads and Pendants of Macramé: Incorporating beads and pendants into macramé projects can add a unique and eye-catching element to your designs. Whether you are creating a bracelet, necklace, or wall hanging, these embellishments can elevate your macramé piece to the next level.

Beads come in a variety of shapes, sizes, and materials, allowing you to customize your macramé project to suit your personal style. From wooden beads to glass beads, there are endless options to choose from. You can opt for beads that match the color scheme of your macramé piece or go for contrasting colors to create a bold and vibrant look. Additionally, beads with intricate patterns or textures can add a touch of elegance and sophistication to your design.

Pendants, on the other hand, are larger decorative pieces that can serve as a focal point in your macramé creation. They can be made from various materials such as metal, gemstones, or even clay. Pendants can be shaped like animals, flowers, or geometric shapes, allowing you to express your creativity and personal style. By incorporating a pendant into your macramé project, you can create a statement piece that is sure to catch the attention of others.

When incorporating beads and pendants into your macramé project, there are several techniques you can use. One common method is to thread the beads onto the cords before starting your macramé knots. This allows the beads to be evenly spaced throughout your design. Alternatively, you can add beads or pendants as you go along, weaving them into the knots or attaching them with jump rings. This technique gives you more flexibility in terms of placement and allows you to create a more organic and free-flowing design.

In addition to adding visual interest, incorporating beads and pendants into your macramé projects can also enhance the functionality of your piece. For example, you can use beads as closures for bracelets or necklaces, making them adjustable and easy to put on and take off. Pendants can also serve as focal points that draw attention to specific areas of your macramé design.

Overall, incorporating beads and pendants into your macramé projects allows you to add a personal touch and create unique and one-of-a-kind pieces. Whether you choose to use beads for their visual appeal or pendants for their functionality, these embellishments can take your macramé creations to the next level.

Advanced Jewelry Techniques and Ideas of Macramé: Advanced Jewelry Techniques and Ideas of Macramé is a comprehensive guide that delves into the intricate world of macramé and its application in jewelry making. This resource is designed for individuals who have a basic understanding of macramé and are looking to take their skills to the next level.

The book begins by providing a brief introduction to macramé, its history, and its relevance in contemporary jewelry making. It explores the various tools and materials required for macramé jewelry, including different types of cords, beads, and findings. The author also discusses the importance of color and texture in creating visually appealing macramé jewelry pieces.

One of the highlights of this book is its focus on advanced macramé techniques. It covers a wide range of knotting techniques, such as the square knot, half hitch knot, and lark's head knot, and provides step-by-step instructions on how to execute them effectively. The author also introduces more complex techniques, such as the Josephine knot, the double half hitch knot, and the Chinese crown knot, which add depth and intricacy to macramé jewelry designs.

In addition to knotting techniques, this book explores various macramé jewelry making techniques, including braiding, weaving, and wrapping. It provides detailed instructions on how to create different types of macramé jewelry, such as bracelets, necklaces, earrings, and rings. The author also offers tips and tricks on how to incorporate beads, charms, and pendants into macramé designs, allowing readers to personalize their creations and make them truly unique.

Furthermore, this book goes beyond technique and provides inspiration for creating stunning macramé jewelry pieces. It showcases a wide range of design ideas, from simple and minimalist designs to more elaborate and statement-making pieces. The author encourages readers to experiment with different color combinations, patterns, and textures, and provides guidance on how to create harmonious and visually appealing compositions.

To enhance the learning experience, this book includes detailed illustrations and photographs that accompany the step-by-step instructions. These visuals not only make it easier for readers to understand the techniques but also serve as a source of inspiration for their own designs.

Overall, Advanced Jewelry Techniques and Ideas of Macramé is a valuable resource for anyone looking to expand their knowledge and skills in macramé jewelry making. Whether you are a hobbyist or a professional jewelry maker, this book offers a wealth of information, techniques, and design ideas that will help you create stunning macramé jewelry pieces.

Understanding Macramé Design Principles of Macramé: Macramé is a versatile and intricate form of textile art that involves knotting cords together to create various patterns and designs. To truly master the art of macramé, it is essential to have a solid understanding of its design principles. These principles serve as guidelines that help artists create visually appealing and balanced macramé pieces.

One of the fundamental design principles in macramé is symmetry. Symmetry refers to the balance achieved by arranging elements in a way that they are evenly distributed on either side of a central axis. In macramé, this can be achieved by using the same knots, patterns, and cords on both sides of the piece. Symmetry creates a sense of harmony and stability in the design, making it visually pleasing to the eye.

Another important design principle in macramé is repetition. Repetition involves using the same knot or pattern multiple times throughout the piece. This creates a sense of unity and coherence in the design. By repeating certain elements, such as knots or motifs, the macramé piece becomes more visually interesting and cohesive.

Contrast is another design principle that plays a significant role in macramé. Contrast refers to the juxtaposition of different elements to create visual interest and variety. In macramé, contrast can be achieved by using different types of knots, varying the thickness or color of the cords, or incorporating different textures. Contrast adds depth and dimension to the macramé piece, making it visually captivating.

Proportion is another crucial design principle in macramé. Proportion refers to the relationship between different elements in terms of size, scale, and placement. It is important to consider the proportions of the cords, knots, and patterns used in macramé to create a balanced and visually pleasing composition. By carefully considering the proportions, artists can ensure that the macramé piece is well-balanced and aesthetically appealing.

Lastly, the design principle of focal point is essential in macramé. A focal point is a specific area or element in the design that draws the viewer's attention. It serves as the center of interest and creates a visual hierarchy within the piece. In macramé, a focal point can be created by using a different knot or pattern, incorporating a unique color or texture, or adding a decorative element. The focal point adds visual impact and directs the viewer's attention to a specific area of the macramé piece.

INTRODUCTION

Macramé is the term used to describe the art of making ornamental knots. It is done by hand, without needles, and involves weaving threads or cords together to form knots that may be simple or complex.

It is a French term that translates as a knot, and it is one of the oldest forms of artistic expression. It is a textile-making method that employs knots to produce a variety of different fabrics and items. Due to the resurgence in popularity of this ancient art form in recent years, artisans are coming up with new and inventive methods to use macramé. This tradition has been in and out of favor for thousands of years, and it continues to do so now. However, due to its usefulness, this technique will continue to be used to some extent indefinitely. Macramé is a flexible type of fiber art used to create various things ranging from wall art and plant holders to jewelry, handbags, and even garments. It is made out of basic materials such as linen, twine, cotton, jute, or yarn, and it can be as basic or as complicated as the maker desires. Amazingly, you can create table runners and key chains with nothing more than your hands and a few cheap materials. Once you have mastered the fundamental macramé knots and methods, you will be prepared to begin working on your first creation. Many of the designs in this book will take you from the beginning of a project to its very finish. The completed item may serve as a trophy for your accomplishments in the arts or as a personal present for a friend who appreciates your work. When it is sold, it may also provide a significant profit. For any macramé project that takes your fancy, it is essential to have all kinds of cords, rings, beads, and other accessories available before you get started. This book includes detail about macramé tools and equipment. Knotting helps to improve your fine motor abilities as well as your bilateral dexterity and agility. Individuals who suffer from joint and muscular discomfort in their hands and fingers may benefit greatly from this practice. With a little bit of effort and patience, your fingers will be working on the project after project in no time at all.

1.
BASICS OF MACRAMÉ

M acramé is a textile-making method that employs knots to produce a variety of different fabrics. Due to the resurgence in popularity of this ancient art form in recent years, artisans and artists are coming up with new and inventive methods to use macramé beyond the traditional plant hangers and wall hangings. This age-old tradition has been in and out of favor for thousands of years, and it continues to do so now. However, due to its usefulness, this technique will continue to be used to some extent indefinitely. Amazingly, you can create table runners and key chains with nothing more than your hands and a few cheap materials. For additional information on how macramé came to be, as well as how you may get started with a macramé craft, please continue reading this book.

Using many knots to create the fundamental structure and function of the item is a technique or way of making a textile that has become popular in recent years. Except for a mounting ring to hold the object in place while you work, no additional tools are needed to complete this project save your own two hands. For anything to be called a macramé, it must have at least one such knot in its design. The majority of these creations are put together using a variety of knotting techniques. In certain instances, macramé components may be combined with other methods like weaving or knitting to create a unique look.

1.1 H.STORY OF MACRAM⬜

Macramé is an Arabic term that translates as fringe, and it derives from the ancient technique of knotting a fringe to a solid cloth in a repeated pattern. Eventually, whole pieces of knotted textiles were produced, each with a unique texture that was ideal for use as altar cloths, church vestments, and doilies, among other things.

The history of macramé is as vibrant and vivid as the cords and beads used to create it. When elevated to the level of an art form, it opens up a plethora of options for a project. Because of the intricacy of the methods used and the abundance of imagination that goes into creating them, the final items may be regarded as works of art by the public.

These items are made by tying the strands together in a certain pattern. Different knots create a pattern, and this pattern of interconnecting knots creates a visual feast, particularly when the item incorporates a plethora of brightly colored cords and beads into the design. On the other hand, if you are interested in understanding where and when this style originated, you will enjoy a little excursion into the history of this wonderful art form.

The early history of macramé is a little hazy at this point. According to historical records, there is some evidence that it was practiced in France and Italy throughout the fourteenth and fifteenth centuries. In France, many such items were created, and historical records indicate that it was regarded as an established art form.

Macramé style was thus very popular in the nineteenth century among British and North American sailors, who would spend their long hours at sea making square and hitch knots to keep themselves entertained. Fringes for wheel, bell covers, nets and screens were all created by sailors. The majority of these knotted items were subsequently traded for money in Indian and Chinese markets after that.

In the late 16th century, Queen Mary is said to have brought macramé to the UK from Holland, where she had mastered the art herself. Queen Charlotte was often seen knotting these fringes for adornments at the court, which she inherited from her father.

In the following years, macramé gained popularity across the globe, and many nations already had some knot tying system in place that they utilized for their indigenous art. The emphasis of Macramé throughout the first half of the twentieth century was on practical items like purses, belts, dog leashes, lanyards, light and shade pulls, and bell pulls; these were all popular during the time.

Local artisans continued to make shawls and handbags as a traditional native craft throughout this period.

Throughout the 1960s and 1970s in America, it became a popular craft among the hippie generation and the children of the '70s, among other groups. In the 1980s, interest in this craft began to wane, and the craft eventually disappeared from memory. No longer the case, since macramé is making a major return with individuals of all ages.

1.2 THE FUNDAMENTALS OF MACRAM□

To get started with Macramé, you'll need to be familiar with certain fundamental concepts. The more confident you are in creating these projects, the more enjoyment you will have as you finish one project after another.

Calculate the Amount of Cord

You'll need to figure out how much cording you'll need and how long it should be in total. Even though most projects will provide you with the required dimensions, you should understand how these measurements are obtained. It is recommended that the ends of the cording be 3 to 4 times longer than the item you want to create; however, since the cording is doubled in half for knotting, it should be measured 6 to 7 times longer than the quantity necessary.

Remember that you don't want to run out of cording and have to add more to the project, so make sure you measure it liberally. It is much preferable to have additional cording on hand than running out and inserting it in an awkward location within the design.

EXAMPLE

For example, if the final length of the project is one yard, you'll want to measure your cording from one end to the other at a distance of seven to eight yards. Then, after each end is doubled for knotting, there will be two ends, each of which will be between 3 and 4 yards in length.

Make a Sampler

A sampler will be necessary for many such projects so that you can see how the cording is knotted and how long it measures before you begin. The length of heavy cording will take up more space in knotting than the length of lightweight cording, so you'll need to account for this in your calculations of how much cord to use.

Make a sampler about 4 inches by 7 inches in size so that you can assess the length of the cording and the number of ends that will be required for the breadth of the design. To figure out how many ends you need, tie 4 of them together in a square knot and measure the breadth of the knot. You should practice with the knots after deciding on the project you want to create so that you know precisely how the cording will tie and judge the texture and appearance.

Add Beads and Other Items

Beads and other embellishments are often used in macramé creations to make them more fascinating and full of creativity. Many wholesalers on the Internet sell beads of various sorts, and you can get them at beading and craft shops and on the internet. Make certain that the holes in the beads are big enough to accommodate the cording being stranded through them. To complete your design, you slip the beads onto the cording between or in the center of the knots.

It's important to search for beads that are one-of-a-kind and distinctive when adding them to a project to stand out in the design. You'll discover beads in various designs, sizes, and forms, including flowers, figures, and enchantments, amongst other elements.

Look for beads that will work well with the design you're currently working with. Make sure to choose beads that have a color and texture that complements the overall design of your creation. Using soft and delicate beads for smaller crafts is preferable, while big, textured beads are preferred for larger creations. Consider taking your time searching for the perfect beads for your creation, and don't be afraid to try out new ideas.

When buying beads for your crafts, the one thing you must be certain of is that the cording will be able to pass through the center of the bead centers. Keep in mind that you'll be using many strands of cording at a time, all of which will need to pass through the bead, so select beads that are big enough to accommodate the cording.

You'll need to be very cautious while you're working the bead into the strands of cording so that it fits into the pattern exactly as instructed in the project's instructions. A sequence of knots is usually used to attach a bead before it is worked into the project. Another series of knots are then used to hold the bead in place once it has been secured.

How to Add Cords?

There may be instants when you want to include cords into your creation. Examples include:

- When you wish to introduce a new shade.
- It is used when you wish to enhance the size of a certain area of the design.
- When one or more cords grow too short to be tied into a knot properly.

It depends on whether you want the cording to be visible or not, as well as the kind of cording you're using if you want to include them. For the cording to be completely undetectable, you'll want to incorporate it into the design by slicing it in at the end of the pattern. This is accomplished by unwinding both ends of the cording that will be connected before joining them together. You may use fabric cement to keep them squeezed together if you want them to remain that way. Then twist the ends of the cording together, allowing the cording joint to dry completely before continuing with your knotting.

Using a T-pin behind the work where the new cord is to be placed, you may create an undetectable way of adding a short cord or a chord of a different color without drawing attention to yourself. Tie the new cord to the pin as if it were a horizontal line, then incorporate it into the knotting as you would any other cord. Later on, the ends may be bonded or weaved in with a needle or by hand.

You may let any more loose ends of the new cording hang freely and then knot them where they are required if the fringe ends of the cording will be part of the texture of the final product and will be completely visible.

Measure the End of Project

Planning is required when it comes to finishing your Macramé project since you cannot just stop the project and risk it unraveling. Once you've determined how long the ends should be, you may cut them to length. When it comes to finishing the cording, there are many possible options, and each project will have its unique set of instructions.

- Wrapping a succession of loose cords is one method of putting an end to a string of them. It is accomplished by taking one of the current wires and wrapping it around the other cords in the same manner.

Other methods for tying off cords include:

- Using an alternate half Hhtch knot as a guide.
- Using a succession of overhand knots, with one knot at the bottom and tying a single knot at the top.
- An overhand knot is used to secure a line of beads in place.
- Unraveling the plies of the end cords and fraying them to create fringe and fraying.

In addition to braiding two or more cords and then tying them together with an overhand knot, there are additional techniques for finishing the job. Two or more wire groups should be twisted together clockwise, then counterclockwise. To keep the twists together, tie an overhand knot around them. Alternatively, you may twist the cording in the same direction as the initial twist until it bends into strange forms.

You may also use a sequence of monkey knots to secure your position. A hitch over a parallel rod may be used to create a sturdy end that is free of hanging cords. Once the ends are brought to the rear of the work and weaved into the knots, the job is finished! After that, you may glue or sew the ends together to make them more secure. In most instances, each project will contain detailed instructions on how to tie off and finish your work in the most effective manner.

Anchor your Project

While you're working on your project, you must maintain it

securely secured in place. You'll want to use an anchor of some kind to keep the rope ends from unraveling. The following are some of the advantages of anchoring your craft:

- Cords are simple to deal with since they do not get knotted.
- You'll keep track of what you're doing and when you're done.
- You'll maintain a consistent level of tension throughout the project.
- You have the option to keep your cords as tight and secure as you want them to be. As a result, macramé work that is consistent and accurate in tightness and size is produced.

Macramé Board

One method for providing stability to your craft is to use a macramé board. Pin the cording ends to the board with safety pins to keep them in place. For your work to be as clean and consistent as possible from the beginning to the project's conclusion, make sure that the ends of the cording are aligned.

Clipboard

You may also use a basic clipboard as an anchor for your cording if you want to save time. A clipboard will enable you to go through the stages of your project while also allowing you to keep the incomplete component while you aren't currently working on it. When you are ready to resume work, the cording will be clean and tidy until you are ready to begin again.

It is simple to use. Just attach the wire beneath the clip, enabling the wires to swing freely from the board. If you're dealing with center wires, you may glue them to the clipboard to keep them from moving about.

Split Ring

It is yet another method of securing your work and anchoring it to the wall. After you've tied your first knot, slide the knot into the hole of the split ring to secure it. Once you've done that, attach the ring to a sturdy item such as a doorknob or a clothes hanger. Many crafts may need you to cut some threads double as long as others, resulting in a tangled mess. Simply looping the fold of cords over the top of the ring will suffice in this situation. To tighten the knots, just take the whole item out of the ring and tighten the knots from there.

Tighten the Knots

To ensure that the ends of your project are securely fastened, you'll need to tighten your project's starting and end knots. Using pliers is a simple and effective method of doing this. Holding each strand of cording with the tip of the pliers, one at a time ensures that it is secure. To tighten the strands of cording, firmly pull the pliers away from the cording. This will help to reinforce your macramé project, ensuring that it remains safe and secure.

Follow a Uniform Pattern

As you get more expertise in this craft, you'll want to put even more emphasis on working consistently and uniformly throughout your project. When you tie your knots, you'll want them to be evenly tensioned and straight horizontally, vertically, and diagonally across the line. In particular, you'll be searching for strong edges and loops that are consistent in size.

Utilizing a macramé board or other anchoring techniques to keep your work secure while you're working is the quickest and most dependable means of achieving this level of accuracy and precision. This board will assist you in maintaining an equal size of your knots and a consistent pattern throughout your project. Prepare to tie your first knot by getting into the habit of securing your work first. You'll quickly discover that your creations will appear more even if the knots are aligned and the same size as one another.

2.

Macramé Equipment And Tools

Macramé is a kind of textile made using knotting methods rather than weaving or knitting, and it is popular in the Philippines. The knots are square and create full-hitch and double half-hitches when tied together. By using just cheap and readily available materials such as cotton, leather, or yarn, the craft is completed with the addition of a variety of beads to embellish the final product.

When it comes to getting started with macramé, you only need a few basic pieces of equipment and materials to get started. Here is a list of them:

- Rings
- T-pins
- Scissors
- Beads
- Crochet hook
- Macramé Boards
- Mounting Cords
- Measuring Tape
- Embroidery Needles

The macramé board is a working surface on which you will place your work to keep it safe. You may buy this board from a craft shop if you want to get started. If there are no such boards available in your local shops, you may purchase one from one of the vendors mentioned in the supplier portion of this book.

T-pins may be found in a sewing and supplies shop or online. In addition, U-pins, which are excellent for anchoring heavier cords to the board, maybe worth investing in. These pins may be found at shops that provide supplies for upholstery jobs.

You'll use the embroidery needle and crochet hook for projects where you'll be adding tiny details to a macramé design to make it seem more polished and finished. In each particular project, you will find detailed instructions for this kind of finishing.

2.1 B. sic Macram☐ Tools

If you are already an enthusiastic beader or crafter, most of the equipment and many of the supplies mentioned are those that you are likely to have on hand in your workbox. You do not need to purchase everything at once since you can always improvise, but using a comparable material or the equipment and tools mentioned is preferable to get the best results.

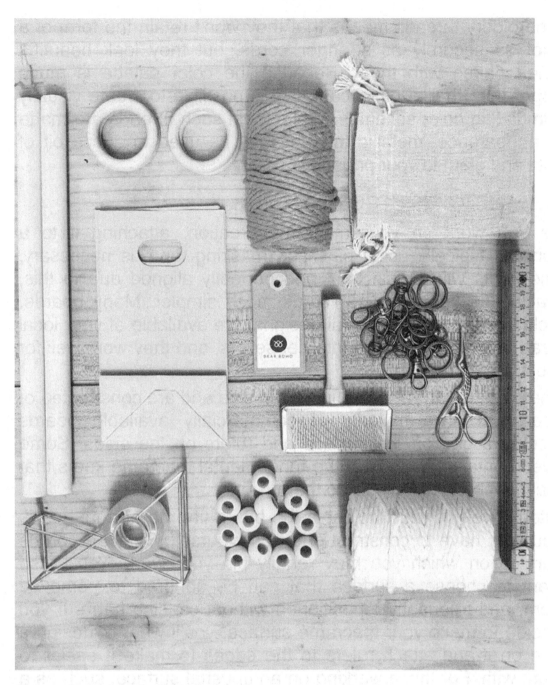

Cords and Threads

It is possible to work with macramé methods in an almost limitless variety of threads and cords. This section discusses the many available options.

Embroidery Threads

Many other threads are used for macramé crafts, but stranded cotton and cotton Perle are often utilized. The softness of embroidery threads means that they won't retain the form of a knot as securely as stronger cords, but they look beautiful when paired with them. Because the color palette is much larger than that of other cables, it is possible to create visually stimulating color schemes. While most such threads are matte in appearance, metallic threads may be used to add a bit of glitz and glam to your projects.

Macramé Boards

As you work on your macramé creation, attaching it to a surface, typically using pins and masking tape, is necessary. The knots will remain tight and perfectly aligned due to this, making dealing with your cords much simpler. Many boards, including those with special designs, are available at your local bead or craft shop or via internet sellers, and they work well for most applications.

They are usually 12 by 18 inches in size and are constructed of fiberboard. The majority of commercially available boards include a grid on the surface and rulers on the sides. Some even contain drawings of the fundamental macramé knots that may teach others how to do them.

Alternatively, if your project is too big to fit on a normal board, you may have to construct one from yourself. Select a porous surface on which you may readily pin your work. You'll also want to choose a surface that can be adhered to, removed from, and frequently repositioned without causing harm. If you decide to make your macramé surface, you'll want to design a grid on it and attach rulers to the edges to make it easier to work with. For those working on an unusual surface, such as a table or an aircraft tray, you may wish to include a piece of tape with dimensions written on it, so you always have a handy reference.

T-pins

Pins and tape are used to hold things together. Using pins, you may keep your project firmly attached to your macramé board so that it doesn't move about while you're working. Moreover, they are useful for keeping specific strands in position while integrating different knot combinations and other design features into your creations.

These pins are the most often used kind of pin for macramé projects. They are a good length, and their form makes it simple to insert and remove them consistently. In addition to these pins, ball-end pins used for sewing may also be used, although they are not nearly as durable as these pins. Pushpins and thumbtacks should not be used instead of staples since they are both too short.

Masking Tape

Masking tape is also used to hold items to your work surface while you are working. However, if you're working on a more sensitive surface, it may serve as a replacement for T-pins. It is, however, most often used to attach cords, which are cords around which you're tying your working cords when making square and twist knots.

Use caution when replacing transparent tape with duct tape. Duct tape, packing and any other clear tape are all excessively sticky and may cause damage to your cables and surface, as well as being very difficult to remove.

Scissors

Most macramé creations are created with thin, simple fibers to cut using a basic pair of craft scissors, such as ones you already possess. When a project is finished, you may wish to get a pair of small trimming scissors specifically intended for sewing to cut the extra length. They'll enable you to get up close and personal with any knots you'd want to cut out.

Some of the crafts in this book call for the use of suede and leather hides, as well as cording. To cut through them, you'll need a more powerful pair of scissors. They are strong enough to handle skins while being tiny enough to cut ends close to knots, and they are also excellent for just about anything else. If you want to deal with these materials regularly, you should get a higher-quality pair of scissors.

Findings

Generally speaking, findings are little bits, often made of metal, used to create and finish jewelry or other accessories. Many of the discoveries are utilized to hide the raw accessories, which is a common practice. Because many of the findings are used to conceal the raw ends of cords, it is critical to choose the right size and form while making your selection. Maintain a diverse collection of findings in your workbox so that you may construct and finish a variety of items.

Cord Ends

When used to finish single wires, some types have lugs that are fastened over the cord using pliers, while others are tubular and are either attached with glue or have an integrated crimp ring secured with adhesive.

Finishing Ends

These embellishments are used to complete the ends of knotted ropes, and they are made of brass. With each passing year, there is an increasing number of models accessible, with the majority of them being offered in a variety of metallic finishes. To get the best results, match the internal dimensions of the finishing ends to the internal dimensions of the cord or braid. Some already have a fastening for finishing ends; however, see jewelry ones for your choices if this is not the case.

Spring Ends

These are some of the most traditional types of discovery, and they may be either cylindrical or cone-shaped. Tuck, the cord or braid inside the wire coil, then use pliers to compress just the end ring of the coil to ensure it is securely fastened.

End Cones

This cone- or bell-shaped finds may be completed with either a hole or a loop at the top of the cone or bell. If possible, use jewelry glue to bind the braid into both styles for the greatest results.

End Caps

Ended cones are available in cylindrical, square, and rectangular shapes. These caps are similar to end cones in that they have a hole at the top or are pre-finished with a hook or ring. If possible, use jewelry glue to bind the braid into both styles for the greatest results.

Adhesives

Most macramé creations are finished by applying glue to the last knot in the chain. The kind of glue to be used will be determined by the materials that are being used. White glue is excellent for use with silk, waxed linen, cotton, and other fibers, among other things.

When working with leather and suede, cement, also known as contact cement, is ideal. A highly strong glue, such as epoxy, is utilized to join nonporous materials together, such as wire or even the labradorite beads used in conjunction with the heart belt buckle.

It is necessary to provide enough ventilation while using these adhesives, and all warning labels should be carefully obeyed. Take the toxicity of glue into consideration when choosing which adhesive to use for your project, particularly if the glue is going to be in direct contact with human flesh.

Wires

It is challenging to work with when making macramé jewelry, but if you learn the technique, the results may be stunningly original jewelry pieces. Metal cannot be bent repeatedly. In addition to being brittle, it becomes work-hardened and brittle after being bent over and over again. If you bend it back and forth again and over again, it will ultimately break.

Furthermore, the heavier wire will not bend without a tremendous amount of effort on the user's part. When it comes to metal macramé, most of it is done using smaller gauge wire, which is simpler to handle. It will retain its stiffness even after being exercised, so the less you bend it, the better.

Ribbon Crimps

This product is intended to cover the raw end of the ribbon, but it may also be used to finish flat braids and wire. To prevent the braid from being damaged, seal the ribbon crimp over the braid using nylon-jaw pliers.

Jewelry Fastenings

Many various types of findings may be used to complete jewelry pieces like chains, ornaments, earrings, and hoops, among other things. End caps have a magnetic fastening built into the design; otherwise, select a style that matches the end cap and complements the color and weight distribution.

Toggle Fastenings

With this two-part fastening, the T-bar and ring are rotated on their sides so that the bar may slide into or out of the ring. As a design element, go for a more ornamental style.

Magnetic Fastenings

The design of these attractive fasteners incorporates a powerful magnet that holds them securely in place. They are ideal for adding a final touch to necklaces and wristbands.

Trigger Clasp

Both wristbands and necklaces may be finished with this low-cost fastener, which has a spring-loaded closing. The lobster claw and bolt ring are two of the available designs.

Multi Clasps

These are available in several different designs. In addition to necklaces, the box form is excellent for bracelets such as macramé and other cuff-style ornaments. Decide on the number of rings on each side that will work best for your project.

Plastic Clasps

These clasps, which feature a bar end to which the cords may be attached, are specifically intended for knotting methods such as macramé. A variety of sizes and vivid colors are available for the clasps.

Beads

Beads may be incorporated into any macramé method in several ways, either during the knotting process or subsequently. The majority of macramé crafts would be incomplete without the addition of beads. The number of bead choices available is mind-boggling. Because of the expansion of international commerce and technological advancements, the variety of beads available to jewelry makers has increased to the point that it is nearly overwhelming. They are of many types as:

- Pearls
- Buttons
- Metal beads
- Bone beads
- Fresh seed beads
- Antique seed beads
- Semiprecious gemstones
- Handcrafted lampwork glass beads

They are available in a variety of colors, shapes, and sizes. When looking for the beads that will be used in your project, one of the essential factors to consider is the size of the holes in the beads. Each bead has to be large enough to fit the materials you want to use to tie the knot with.

If you cannot thread your material through the bead's hole, the hole will need to be expanded, which will require more time and effort than you are prepared to devote. It may be helpful to bring a sample of the material you want to use to the bead or craft store when you go shopping. Instead, the wire wrap project modification provides a more creative solution for issues with large beads and tiny holes. If you find yourself with a collection of beads with holes that are so tiny that they seem to be worthless, you may use them to make the belt buckle for the leather belt project etc.

2.2 HOW TO CHOOSE THE RIGHT CORDS?

Once you have mastered a method, you should experiment with various materials to see what you come up with. You will be astonished by the outcomes. Knots can lose definition when working with a soft cord such as rattail or cotton, but the form may be more apparent when handled with a stronger cord-like Superlon or wax cotton or when using a circular leather thong.

Before you begin, think about how you want the final object to appear and choose the cord or thread that best suits your vision.

It's important to remember that each of these cords is available in various thicknesses and maybe worked individually or in groups of many bundles.

Cord Guide

This sample board of cords allows you to see some of the appropriate cords for macramé and provides a fast reference to the variety of thicknesses available in the various cable types.

Rattail Cord

In addition to having a high sheen, this silky cord is also available in various thicknesses:

- Bucktail-1mm
- Mousetail-1.5mm
- Rattail -2mm

As it is very soft, it does not hold the form of knots very well, nor does it have a particularly long lifespan.

Chinese Cord

When working with this nylon braided cord, it retains its round appearance. The finer cords, now available in diameters ranging from 0.5mm to 3mm, are usually more popular for macramé crafts. Look online for the most comprehensive color selections; nevertheless, you may discover that the color selection for thicker cords is less broad than the color selection for finer cords.

Wax Cotton Cord

This cord may be used for a variety of different methods. Keep an eye out for a 3mm string, which is especially useful for individual knots and tied braids since it maintains its form better and is more durable. A thinner cord is excellent for macramé projects since it is easier to thread beads through.

They are available in various natural hues and various colors, many of which are in keeping with current fashion trends. Remove kinks and restore the polish to this cord that has become soft from usage or that you wish to reuse by pulling through under a hot iron for several minutes.

Superlon

It is a twisted nylon cord of industrial strength that was initially used for upholstery applications. 0.6mm and 0.8mm widths are also available, and both are ideal for micro macramé and other knotting methods where a tiny braid or finish is desired.

These cords are ideal for incorporating beads into your knitting, and they may be combined with thicker cords to create a different feel. There are a variety of neutrals and beautiful modern colors to choose from to suit your taste.

Paracord

This cord has two typical thicknesses:

- 550 (4mm), which has seven strands.
- 450 (2mm), which has four center strands.

The bulkiness of this cord makes it ideal for creating bracelets and other accessories from single knots, and it is particularly popular for men's jewelry due to its ease of use. In addition to a variety of solid bright, and dark colors, the cable is also available in many different multicolored patterns to suit your style.

Leather Thong Cords

It is a strong cord, and a round leather thong creates an excellent distinguishing knot. It is available in a variety of thicknesses ranging from about 0.5mm to 5mm. Thinner cords are better for tying knots, whereas thicker cords are better for using as a core around which to tie the knots.

A variety of colors and natural hues of leather are available in thongs for women. The various thicknesses of snakeskin effect cords, typically in light pastels, are very appealing, as are pearlescent finishes usually in pale pastels.

Faux Suede Cords

It has the appearance of genuine leather suede, but it is considerably more flexible than the real thing and gives knots a different appearance than they would otherwise have. It is typically a 3mm broad and is available in various colors, depending on the manufacturer.

2.3 HOW TO CHOOSE THE RIGHT BEADS?

Beads are available in various colors, finishes, sizes, and forms, but the size of the hole is critical for knotting since it allows the beads to be readily strung onto the string. When you go bead shopping, it is good to bring a cord sample with you to try on.

Seed Beads

This general word refers to the little glass beads used mainly for bead stitching and stringing. Basic seed beads are donut-shaped, and the most common sizes are 1 to 5.5mm, with 1mm being the smallest; cylinder-shaped beads, also known as delicas, have larger holes and can be strung on a 1 to 2mm cord.

Keep an eye out for beads with unique textures, such as:

- Hex beads
- Papillon beads
- Charlotte beads
- Triangular beads
- Magatamas beads

Large beads

Many various types of beads may be used in knotting methods, ranging from basic wood beads to beautiful pearls and crystals, and the decision is entirely up to you. The size of the bead hole does not have to be a constraint since the decision is yours. Because certain beads have unexpectedly big holes, such as those in the Swarovski bead line, even the largest 5 or 6mm beads may be strung on 1mm thread, you are not limited by the size of the beads' holes. Pandora beads have very wide holes and can be strung on cords up to 5mm in diameter.

Focal Beads

These extra-large beads are often utilized as the main point of a piece of jewelry because of their size. You may use bail to hang pendant beads or connect cords to big ring beads to create designs. Additionally, keep in mind that big beads may be strung together using two pieces of macramé that have been completed with end caps.

2.4 MACRAM MATERIAL

Macramé is a kind of textile art that employs several different types of cording to create its designs. If you want to make these items, the yarns and cording you use should be sturdy enough to withstand the abrasion throughout the knotting process. They should not have a lot of elasticity or give to them. Also, you want to choose a cording that will maintain its identity so that the knots can be readily identified in the final product.

When it comes to Macramé crafts, the knotting pattern is critical, and you want each knotting segment to be distinct and readily distinguishable from the others. Most of the time, when you're creating these projects that you'll be wearing, you'll want to choose a cording that will be pleasant against your skin. For example, while making chains, wristbands, anklets, and other such projects that you'll be wearing. The tension and strength of cording are important characteristics to look for in other tasks, such as plant hanger making. You'll need to consider the weather while selecting cording for any such creations that will be shown outdoors.

Fortunately, most macramé designs will provide you with recommendations on the kind of material that would work best for the pattern, so you won't have to rely on intuition when it comes to the cording. Cords may be constructed of natural materials or synthetic materials such as:

- Silk
- Flax
- Jute
- Wool
- Raffia
- Manila
- Hemp
- Sisal
- Nylon
- Cotton
- Linen
- Plastic
- Rayon
- Polyethylene

Cords are measured by their diameter and weight. The diameters will range from a quarter of an inch to three-quarters of an inch and thicker. A large number of balls of cording will be sold by the pound at a specified price per pound. Each project that you work on will specify the size of the cording that should be used to get the greatest possible final result.

Cotton

Its fibers are shorter than jute, hemp, or linen fibers, and they need a greater amount of twisting to remain together and create a strand of fabric. Depending on where you reside, cotton cording may be purchased from most fabric and sewing shops and weaving providers. Single-ply cotton is often chosen for macramé items worn, like a belt, since it is more durable. Cotton cording is available in a broad range of diameters and is often used in Macramé crafts due to its versatility.

Jute

It is an excellent material for a wide variety of macramé crafts. It is not too expensive, and the yarn thickness ensures that you will see results quickly. It is available in a variety of thicknesses, ranging from 2 to 5-ply. When working with jute, one thing to bear in mind is that it is not colorfast. This implies that if you're utilizing it in a project exposed to electric or natural light for a long period, it will begin to fade with time.

You'll discover that the natural tone of this material, which is a sandy, light-colored brown, will work well for natural projects in which you'll be including things like shells, stones, natural beads, and other rustic elements into your design. In addition to natural material, colored jute is also available for those macramé applications that need color. Alternatively, you may take your project to the next level by dyeing your jute.

Hemp

These cords are favored over other fiber cords for making macramé jewelry. This is because it knots readily and retains its shape effectively. It is smooth enough to be worn pleasantly on the skin, making it an excellent material for jewelry-making projects of many kinds. Even though jute cord is quite similar to hemp ones, jute is much too rough for macramé jewelry-making tasks.

It is available in several different sizes and finishes. This covers anything from thread-weight to thick hemp rope and everything in between. It is naturally a medium brown hue, but you may purchase a jewelry-weight one dyed in several colors if you want a different look.

Linen

This cording is available in a broad range of colors and weights, making it a popular choice for a wide range of knotting designs and applications. The fabric has the strength and versatility that many other kinds of cording lack, making it an excellent choice for Macramé projects that need a high level of strength and endurance. The use of linen cording in wall hangings is common, and it looks particularly well when paired with other kinds of cording, such as cotton and silk.

One thing to keep in mind is, this cording tends to fray quickly, so you'll want to take extra care to finish up the ends of your creation with precision. While color is unique to each of us, and our response to color may change depending on our mood, there are a few color factors that you should bear in mind while designing your next project.

When Working with Color

In cases when a macramé creation is intended to mix various textures via the use of an elaborate knotting pattern, it is generally preferable to utilize a single color throughout. To avoid the beads from glistening and detracting from the simplicity of the knitting pattern, you may want to make sure that they are integrated into the design as part of the overall design.

It is possible to add color and depth to a project by cording in more than one color. It is possible to include cords of a different color into a knotting design by following these steps:

- Unraveling the end of the cord that has already been worked into the pattern and the end of the new cord of a different color.

- Dip each end into the fabric cement and connect them, allowing the cement to dry fully before repeating the knotting pattern on the other end.

- Use T-pins to tie the new color that will be introduced into the project onto the board that will be attached to the wall behind the work.

- Then weave the fresh string into the design using an embroidery needle, returning later to finish the job with an embroidery needle.

Once you complete your first project that incorporates several colors of cording, you'll be amazed at how simple the technique is. Even the simplest macramé craft will become more interesting as you experiment with different color combinations.

3.

LEARNING MACRAMÉ KNOTS

A macramé is simply a sequence of knots that are tied in a certain pattern. The following knots will teach you all that you need to know to get started. Create a sampler before you begin working on any such project to practice the knots used in the pattern before working on the item. The square and the half-hitch are the only knots you need to know. The variations and combinations of these two knots will account for about 90% of all the knots used in this process.

3.1 B. SICS OF MACRAM☐ KNOTTING

If you are familiar with the terminology frequently used in knotting, you will find that the directions for creating knots are much simpler to follow. Also, it is good to get familiar with the fundamental knots used in macramé crafts before beginning to learn any advanced methods.

Did you know that there are some distinct kinds of knotting, even though we often use the term knot to refer to all of them?

- To connect two separate cords, use a bend knot.
- To connect one cord around another item, use a hitch knot.
- To connect one or both ends of a cord around itself, use a knot
- To connect one or both ends of a cord around itself, use a stopper one.

Knotting Terminology

Take a minute or two to get acquainted with the knotting language often used in step instructions to make your life easier.

- The end of the wire used to tie the knot is referred to as the working end.
- If you start in the center of a chord, both ends will be working ends.
- If you start in the middle of a cord, both ends will be functioning ends.
- The crossing point is a point at which one string crosses over the other.
- When the working end is on top of the cross point, it is called an overhand point.
- When the working end is below, it is called an underhand point.
- Firm up means to tighten the knot until the cords are securely fastened, but not so tightly that the knot becomes deformed.
- Looping the working end clockwise and repeatedly is referred to as an overhand loop in certain circles.
- The cord is coiled after being wrapped around one or more strands numerous times.
- An anticlockwise loop is also known as an underhand loop. This is a technique in which the working end is wrapped around anticlockwise and over itself twice.
- A U-shaped bend is also known as a bight. This is a kind of knot commonly used to weave the thread through the knot as it is being tied.
- The knot is circled because the cord is wrapped around one or more strands.
- Weave means to pass consecutive cords over and under one another in a knot with a working end or a U-shaped bend.

- A core cable is a cord that is permanently embedded inside other threads and cords. Macramé is a technique in which the core cords may be transformed into working cords and vice versa.

- Often used to create the fundamental shape, a base cord may also replace a finding such as a solid ring, clasp, or bar.

- Most of the time, the lark's head knot connects the working cable to the base cord.

3.2 How to Tie Different Knots?

Macramé is a beautiful knotting art that anybody can learn to perform with a little bit of effort and patience. It's a fantastic method to turn your ideas into beautiful and useful works of art that will add a touch of old flair to your house. It is a simple craft to master. Even though it seems to be a difficult craft, it is a basic craft that anybody can learn to perform at first sight. Once you've mastered the fundamental knots, you may combine them in various ways to create any design you can envision.

Square Knot

This knot is the most common kind of knot and is the most often used. It is usually made with a minimum of two cords, referred to as the knotting cords. Filler ones are defined as one or more cords that are located in the middle of the loom. The rust strands are the knotting cords, and the brown cords are the fillers.

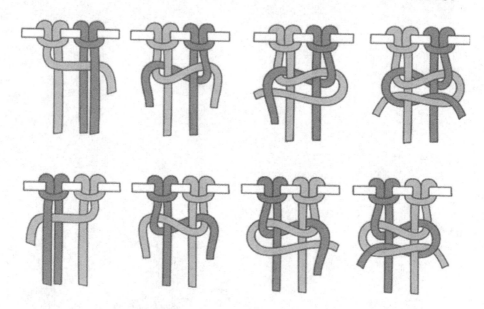

- Begin with four cords and work your way up from there.
- Firstly place the left cord over the two fillers and beneath the right cord.
- Afterward, pass the appropriate cord behind the fillers and through the loop.

- Next, take the right cord and put it over the two fillers and under the left cord. This completes the design.
- To complete the loop, we pass the left cord under the fillings and through it. This brings the square knot to a close.
- Whenever you tighten the knots, it is good to pull at the cords from a distance.
- If all of the knots are the same size, the project will have a more uniform appea rance.

HOW TO ANCHOR IT?

- Cross the left anchor cord across and to the right of the two anchor cords to complete the loop.
- Cross the right one across the left cord to complete the loop.
- Thread the right one through the loop created by the left cord and beneath the anchors.
- The first half of the knot is formed by pulling on the other half of the Knot.
- Cross the right cord over and to the left of the two anchor cables, and then cross the right cord over the left chord again.
- Thread the left cord through the loop created by the right cord and beneath the anchors.
- Pull the strands together, and you'll have the completed Square Knot on your hands.

Once you've mastered this knot, you'll be able to create a variety of patterns by combining other knots. A sinnet is a group of two or more such knots tied together with the same filler.

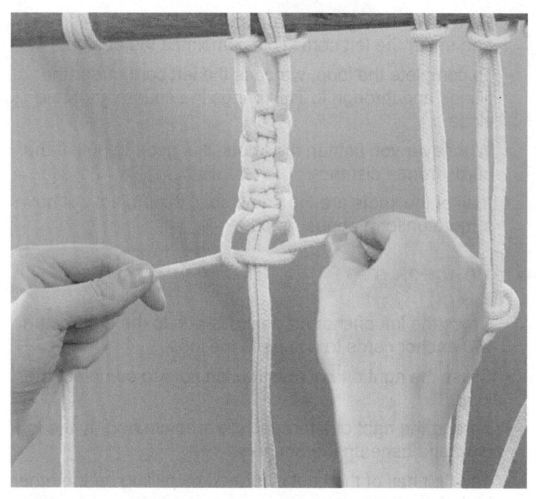

Overhand Knot

This knot is one of the macramé's simplest and most adaptable knots. Most of the time, it is used to start or finish a macramé piece.

- Make a loop with the cording and tie it off.
- Wrap one end of the cording from around the cord through the loop and tighten the knot with your fingers.

Half Knot

This knot may be tied from right to left or left to right, depending on your preference.

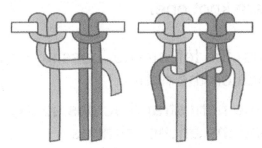

- Begin with four cords and work your way up from there.
- Cross the left anchor cord across and to the right of the two anchor cords to complete the loop.
- Cross the right one across the left cord to complete the loop.
- Thread the right one through the loop created by the left cord and beneath the anchors.
- Tighten the knot until it is completely closed.

Square Knot Sinnet

This is a kind of sinnet in which the outside strands of cording are worked. There can be no anchor strands, one, two, or more anchor strands present.

- Tie a square knot with the left strand crossing in front of the anchor strands on both sides.
- Tuck the right strand under the anchor strands, ensuring that the anchor strands are completely contained in a loop.
- Tie a second knot with the right strand crossing in front of the left strand.
- Tighten the grip.

Half Knot Sinnet

This is a spiral made of half knots. This knot creates the appearance of a flat twisted ribbon and is constructed in the same manner as a square knot one.

- Tie a half knot with the left strand, passing it in front of the anchor strands on the right.
- Secondly, bring the right strand across so that it passes behind and behind the anchor strands.
- At this stage, the anchor strands are looped together to form a secure connection.
- Repeat the process.
- As the sinnet increases in size, the knots will begin to form a spiral.

Half Hitch Knot

In this knot, a single wrap of one strand around another strand creates a secure connection. Bring the end of the cord up between the working and anchor strands and tighten the knot.

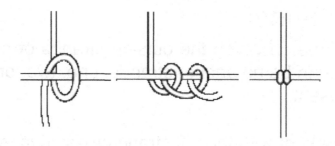

- Tie a macramé cord around a knitting needle and fasten it.
- Tuck the small end of it beneath the larger length of the cord to secure it.
- Thread the short end of the cord through the hole between where the cord crosses and the needle, and then back up through the hole.

- Pull it tight around the knot and through the needle.

This macramé knot is simple, but it is one that you will find yourself doing fairly often. Therefore it is one that you should invest the necessary time in learning to perform evenly.

Half Hitch Spiral

- Tie a sequence of half hitch knots around the other strand to form a spiral using one strand.
- Continue this process until you get the required length of the spiral.

Vertical Double Half Hitch

This is tied from left to right or right to left, depending on the direction of the knot. Over a vertical anchor cord, the rope is tied in a knot.

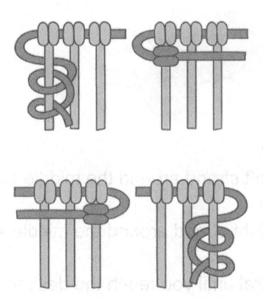

Horizontal Double Half Hitch

This is tied from left to right or right to left, depending on the direction of the knot. The cord is knotted over a horizontal anchor cord to provide a secure connection.

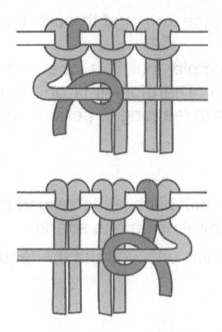

Alternating Half Hitch Knot

In this knot, a variant of the half hitch is used. Instead of a spiral, a flat sinnet is produced by this method.

- Half-hitch the left strand around the middle strand twice more than once.
- Half-hitch the right strand around the middle strand twice.
- Continue to spiral until you reach the desired amount of time.
- As you work, straighten the knots with your fingertips to make them easier to deal with.

Double Half Hitch Knot

- A double half hitch is made by wrapping the left chord around the two center cords and back through itself, then wrapping it around and over again.

- The right cord then loops around the two center cords and back through itself before looping again on the left.

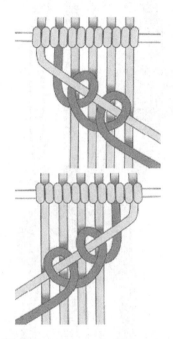

Alternating Square Knot

It comprises eight strands of cording and is similar to the square knot. The result of this knotting design is a delicate and lacy appearance. Make sure not to tighten the knots too tight while you're working them to keep the lacy appearance. Separate the strands and secure them so that they are next to each other on the bed.

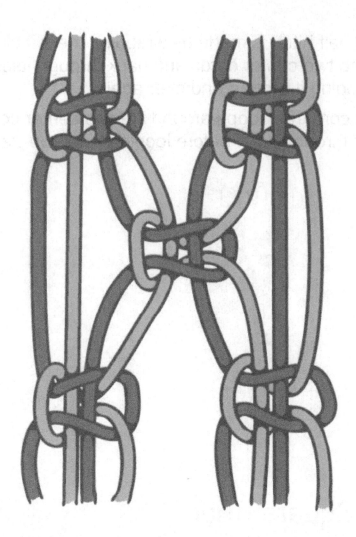

- Separate the strands into two groups of four each.
- In each group, make a square knot by crossing the two outside strands over the two center strands and tying the knot.
- To make a center, bring the two left strands of the right group and two right strands of the left group together to the center, dropping the two outside strands on each side of the center.
- Create a knot by crossing the two outside strands over the two center threads and tying the knot.
- With this, one unit of the knot is completed.
- Continue from step 1 until you have reached the desired length.

Josephine Knot

This beautiful knot looks best when used in long, lacy patterns with many hair strands. This knot has a highly distinct and one-of-a-kind appearance.

- Make a loop with the strands on the left.
- Put the right strands over the loop and slip the right strands under the loose strand ends on the left side of the loop.
- Slide the thread ends over the top left threads and weaves the thread diagonally around the loop, starting at the left end.
- Strengthen the knot evenly all the way around.

Lark's Head Knot

This is a knot that is often used to connect cords to a holding or starting line.

- Fold the string in half and put the loop beneath the horizontal holding line from top to bottom, starting at the top and working your way down.
- Bring the two loose strands down through the loop by reaching beneath and over the horizontal line.
- Pull-on the knot to tighten it.

Alternating Lark's Head Knot

This is a more stylish variation of Lark's knot that may be worn as a necklace. This knot gives you more flexibility when it comes to using loops for decorating.

- Starting on either the left or right side of the cording, tie a Knot around the anchor strands, using the outer strand of the cording as the anchor.

- Drop the strand and take up the outer strand on the other side to form another knot.
- Repeat step 3 on alternate sides until you reach the desired length of the scarf.

Chinese Crown Knot

It is a kind of knot that is used to tie a bow. Intricate in its design, this knot seems to be a box on one side and a cross on the other when correctly tied in the right manner.

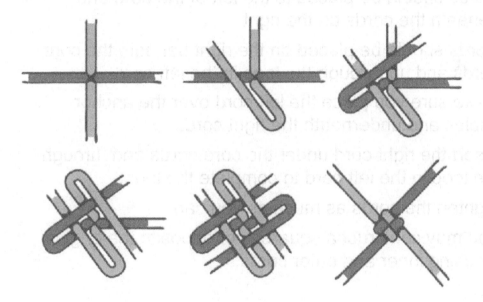

- Form R shape with the right strand by wrapping it under and around the left cord.
- Pull the strand on the left behind you, up and through the top of the knot.
- Fold the strand down over the front of the knot and secure it with your fingers.
- Pass the right strand through the bottom left loop and across the front of the work.

Reverse Square Knot

It entails using the outer ones as working cords and the inner ones as core cords in the same manner.

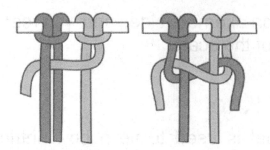

- Cords should be placed to the left of the core and beneath the cords on the right.

- Cords should be placed on the right beneath the core cords and up through the loop in the left cord.

- Make sure you place the left cord over the anchor cables and underneath the right cord.

- Insert the right cord under the core cords and through the loop in the left cord to complete the loop.

- Tighten the cords as much as you can.

- You may construct a square knot opposite the original by using inner and outer cords.

Braided Lark's Head Knot

This is similar to the alternating lark's braid, except that you use four cords instead of two.

- Take the right string and pass it over the filler strings, creating a loop to the left and bringing it through to the front.

- Then, using the same string, pass it under the filler strings, making a loop to the left and passing it through to the front.

- To finish, take a right string and pass it over the filler strings, creating a loop to the right and bringing it through to the front.

- Then, pass it under the filler strings using the same string, creating a loop to the right and bringing it through to the front.

- Keep the knots as near and as tight as possible.

- When the center ones cross, ensure that the left chord crosses over the right cord or the right cross over the left cord.

3.3 TIPS FOR BEGINNERS

If you are a novice or beginner to the art of macramé, the following basic guidelines will assist you in avoiding errors and getting up and running in your new endeavor. Knotting is the most important part of such crafts, but before you get started, here are some pointers that can save you time and aggravation when you are just getting started with the craft.

- Learn how to tie the fundamental knots using hemp rope, which is easy to work with and simple to undo.

- Once you've mastered the fundamentals of knotting, nylon cording should be used for your first few jewelry creations rather than silk.

- It's far simpler to undo knotting errors than it is to prevent them. Singeing the ends of nylon cording is the only method that works.

- Simple project boards may be used as a work surface if you follow these instructions. It's simple to construct and can be transported anywhere, making your project very portable.

- The board should be thick enough to prevent pins from passing through it, and it may be anything from a cushioned board to a corkboard to a piece of polyurethane foam.

- Double-check that the string you want to use will fit through the bead holes you have created.

- Tie a knot at the end of the cord to prevent the ends from fraying. The ends of the cords may also be stiffened by painting them with clear nail polish to prevent them from fraying. This will make it simpler to thread those small seed beads on the cords as well.

- To accomplish the same result, you may also use a no-fray solvent purchased at fabric shops.

- Keep any leftover cording in a container to use for practicing new knots.

- The consistent knotting of your item is essential to achieving a finished appearance. Practice makes perfect, as they say.

- If you don't have any t pins on hand, you may attach your work using corsage pins instead.

- To avoid puncturing the leather cording, create an x with two pins to hold the cord in place and prevent it from slipping. To hold the wires in place, put the pins on each side of the cord, crossing diagonally like an X.

- Always make sure you have a decent pair of fabric scissors available since a large amount of rope may be difficult to cut all at once when you come down to cutting it.

- A strong comb is also helpful for brushing out the fringe on a dress.

- Always cut more cable than you anticipate would be required.

While knotting, you should be mindful of your posture since your back may get sore, particularly after a large job. Invest in a clothes rack that is adjustable; it will be easy on your back. Also, cotton fibers tend to spread around the workspace, so work in a well-ventilated location. The essential things to remember are to allow oneself to study and explore as much as possible since it is a lot more enjoyable method to learn and be creative.

Patience is needed to undo knots and rectify errors. It's better to start with the fundamentals of knotting. Knowing how to tie only one kind of knot, such as the square knot, opens up the possibility of creating many other things. Besides the larks and hitch knot, there are many more excellent knots to master as a beginner.

4.

MACRAMÉ PATTERNS AND TECHNIQUES

Macramé is believed to have originated as a method of tying or creating beautiful fringing on carpets or woven blankets, among other things. The three fundamental knots are used to produce a broad variety of braids, flat panels, and tubular structures. Even though there are only three basic knots, they may be used individually or in combination to make a large variety of braids, flat panels, and tubular structures.

To distinguish it from other knotted braids, which are often handled with the hands, macramé is frequently fastened to a work table using pins or a spring clip. The square and half-knot done with three or four cords are simple to learn, and after you have mastered them, you may go to multistrand methods and various applications of the half-knot.

4.1 P. ACTICE MACRAM☐ PATTERNS

It is preferable to work on a cork pinboard or a piece of foam core to attach the cables with short map pins that you may use to secure the cables is something to consider. Starting with a loop is a good idea.

- Fold a piece of cord in half and wrap it over a map pin to finish the project.

- A spring clip at the bottom of the board is used to hold the ends together.

- Tuck a second piece of cord under the core cords and tie an overhand knot in the center of the working cord to complete the knotting process.

- To get a better finish on the front side, flip the overhand knot to the reverse position and begin tying the first macramé knot from the reverse position.

- The cords may be taped to a hard work surface for extremely basic braids to make them easier to weave.

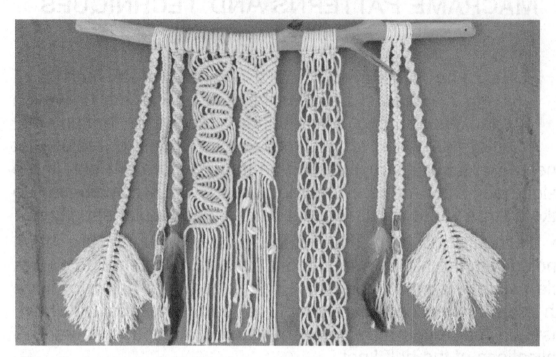

To connect cords to a ring, pendant, or another fastening, tie a lark's head knot around them. You may add a second set of cables, either side by side or nested, to make it even more complicated. An overhand knot may also be used to connect a second pair of cords if you want.

4.2 SQUARE KNOT VARIATIONS

The square knot is a popular knot for creating macramé bracelets and other paracord accessories, and the flat knot braid that results from this knot is known as a Solomon bar. Many beautiful variants may be created by experimenting with various methods to manipulate the basic square knot.

Crossed Cords

Combining two different colors of square knot cords to produce a cross-stitch appearance, with a running stitch pattern on the opposite side.

- Start with a simple overhand knot and work one square knot before firming up the knot.

- Then, fill the ends of a contrast cord color through the square knot beneath the core cords and tie the knot securely.

- Cross the right-hand contrast cord over the left-hand contrast cord and drop the tails on each side of the core cords to complete the design.

- The first half of the next square knot should be worked as follows; the left-hand cord should be passed under the core cords and over the right-hand cord, the right-hand cord should be passed over the core cords and down through the loop on the left-hand cord.

- Raise the contrast cords above the knots a little bit. The second part of the square knot is completed by looping the right-hand cord through the contrast cords but over the core cords and the left-hand cord. The left-hand cord should be threaded beneath the contrast cords but over the core cords before being threaded through the right loop.

- Steps 2–4 should be repeated many times to create a pattern of crosses. Each time, you may cross the right chord across the left cable or alternate the cords for a new effect.

- Keep the contrast cords going down either side of the braid rather than making a cross at step 2 to produce a running stitch pattern on both sides of the braid.

Woven Square Knot

The impact of this is weaved through the center of the braid as it is worked over the fundamental four strands of the braid. It's important to pay attention to the step instructions since the cords are not tied in a simple square knot.

- Make an overhand knot and rotate it to the other side. Transverse the left-hand cable over the left core cord, under the right core cord, then back over the left-hand cord to complete the move.

- Thread the right-hand cable through all of the cords and up through the left loop. Pulling the ends together can help to stiffen them up.

- The right-hand cord should be inserted under the right core cable, over the left core cord, and under the left-hand cord. Afterward, thread the left-hand cord through all of the cables and up through the right loop.

- Continue to repeat the steps until the braid has reached the desired length.

- Make a normal square knot at the end to complete the look.

- The examples are made of paracord, and you may experiment with different thicknesses and widths of the cord to make your patterns.

4.3 MULTI-STRAND MACRAM□ PATTERNS

Macramé may be made with many more cords than the original four, allowing you to construct larger bands for fringe, a belt, or a cuff bracelet by combining the different cords. Depending on the design, multistrand macramé may also be done in the round to create things like purses or plant holders. However, when dealing with more than four cords, you must prepare ahead of time, determining the design, the number of cords needed, and the best way to attach them before you begin.

Alternating Square Knots

It is possible to work a square knot over a single cord (a total of three cords), but it is preferable to work with multiples of four base cords when working with alternating square knots.

- Set up the macramé cords. The cords have been doubled over and fastened to a board. Tying a second-string around each pair of cords using an overhand knot, then rotating the knots for a cleaner finish.

- With the first 4 cords, make a square knot; tie another square knot with the following four cords. Start at one end of the row and work your way across the cords, tying a square knot on each set of four cords until you reach the other end. Maintain the tightness of the knots to prevent them from coming undone.

- The working cords from the preceding row will be transformed into the core cords on the next row and vice versa. To begin, separate the first two cables and move them to the right-hand side of the room. Separate the remaining four strands and tie them together with a square knot.

- Begin working your way across the cords, tying a square knot on each set of four cords, and continuing until you reach the last two cords on the left-hand side.

- A spare cord and a second cord are carried down to the next row. As with the previous row, work the following row from right to left, tying a square knot on the first four cords and every other four cords across the row as you go.

- To finish creating the macramé panel, continue to repeat the two-row tying pattern for a total of four rows. Create an even panel by tying knots at the same spacing each time and using pins to support the panel as you make your way down the panel.

Working with Multiple Cords

Set up your cords for working by starting with loops or by connecting the cords to a fastener, buckle, or another fitting before you start working. One of the benefits of working on a cork pinboard or foam core is that the pins can be used to space out the knots as you go along and to attach cords at an angle to create a more accurate piece of knotting as you go along.

Half-Hitch Ribs

The half-hitches are often worked in pairs as a double half-hitch, and they are typically worked over one of the side cords to create a thick horizontal rib, as seen in the diagram.

- Lay one of the outside strands over the other cords horizontally to create a cross. Draw up and over the horizontal cord, then back under it to the right-hand side with the new outer vertical cord in place.

- Take the same cord and cross it over the horizontal cord, this time bringing it out to the right-hand side through the loop on the other side.

- Repeat the two knots with each of the vertical cords, in turn, to form a thick rib by repeating the process with each vertical cord in turn.

- When you get to the finish, pull the inner cable back across the vertical cords and repeat the procedure in the other way until you reach the beginning.

Angled Half-Hitch Rib

Half-hitches are often used in the construction of panels with shaped sides. The edge of a straight half-hitch is formed by moving one side cord back and forth; however, if you use consecutive cords on a specific side, the edge will be angled.

- Cross the right-hand cable over the other vertical cords and secure it in place. One row of half-hitch rib should be worked across this core cord, tying double half-hitches with each vertical cord to finish the rib.

- Pinch the next right-hand chord across the ribcage and beneath the ribcage.

- Begin by stitching a row of half-hitch rib over the new core cord and ending with a double half-hitch over the previous core cord on the left-hand side.

- Pin the next right-hand cord across under the rib and stitch another row of half-hitches. The panel is now beginning to take on a more angular form on the diagonal.

- Keep in mind to work half-hitches over the preceding core cord at the end of each row to complete the pattern.

- Take the current core chord and pin it back across the vertical cords, towards the right-hand side, to produce a piece of macramé that zigzags in the other way.

- Steps 1 and 2 should be repeated, but each row is working with the next left-hand cord across this time.

4.4 HALF-HITCH VARIATIONS

Using half-hitch ribs, you may create a diagonal pattern by working them at an angle. You can also use them to construct patterns such as leaves and flowers. However, although the double half-hitch is the most often used in macramé methods, it is also feasible to make knotted patterns with single half-hitches.

Diagonal Half-Hitch

The core cord is pinned straight across; however, if the core cord is placed at an angle, a diagonal rib is formed.

- Half-hitch rib should be worked across the cords in one row. Insert a pin at the end of the rib to hold it in place. Form an angled shape by wrapping the side (core) cord around the pin and across the vertical cord at the angle you wish to achieve. Insert a pin to keep the core cord in place.

- Half-hitches should be tied twice with each vertical cord, in turn, being careful to maintain the diagonal line of the rib in mind as you tighten the knots up. Check to see that the vertical cords above the diagonal rib are not too loose or too tight and flat on the body.

- If you want to make a zigzag, just pin the core cord diagonally in the opposite direction of the zigzag and make half-hitches with all of the vertical cords once again. Turn around and repeat the process another way at the end of the row, using the same core cord.

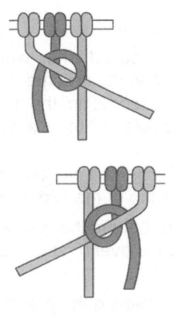

Flower and Petal Patterns

Using half-hitch ribs, it is easy to construct various basic forms with a little forethought. It has been achieved here via the combination of an angled rib and spacing; this method may be used to produce a variety of different designs.

- Pin the right-hand core cord, then take it across the vertical cords and pin it such that the core cord has a small upwards curve on the right-hand side of the cable. Work half-hitches throughout the length of the string, adjusting each knot to keep the curve in place.

- To create the petal form, wrap the core cord on the left around a pin and cross it over the vertical cords in a downwards curve. Complete the petal form by tying half-hitches around the core cord.

The sculptural nature of half-hitches allows the method to create jewelry with a strong sense of structure. Sections of this beautiful piece of macramé with additional beads might be made into a pendant or a necklace, but when worked over a metal rod, it becomes a stunning brooch or hair clip that is sure to turn heads.

Ending Falls Pattern

Single half-hitch variants are called after waterfalls because they have the impression of vertical cords flowing over and falling behind horizontal crosscords in the first of the single half-hitch variations, which is referred to as a waterfall.

- Fold one cord in half around a pin, ensuring that the U-shaped bend is at the top of the folded cord.

- Place the second cord behind the first, and starting at its midpoint, cross the ends over, first to the left and then to the right, so they overlap.

- Make a half-hitch knot behind the crossed-over (beige) cords by pulling the vertical cords up one at a time and tying them so that the tails end facing down in between the knots.

- Continue crossing cords and tying half-hitches until the braid is as long as you want it to be in step 3.

- Pulling on the crossed cords lightly will help to tighten up the half-hitches a little.

- To create a quick and simple bracelet, adjust the top loop to the proper size for a toggle or button fastening loop at the bottom of the wristband.

Side Ending Falls Pattern

To produce a strong stripe along the length of this unending falls variant, the two cord colors are knotted together slightly differently from the other.

- Insert your right-hand end over the left-hand end of one cable and make a loop in the center of it. Place the second cord over the loop above the cross point, just above the cross point.

- Using the right-hand end of the loop cord, wrap it around the loop and pull it out through the newly created loop on the right, securing the second cord (beige) in the process. Pull the first string to tighten the slip knot, then alternate the colors of the cords to create a rainbow effect.

- Work in the same manner as for Endless Falls, but make sure that the vertical colors on each side of the braid are distinct. The crossing ropes will be switched from one side to the other.

Infinite Falls Pattern

The infinite falls are linked together like a chain. Four or more vertical cords are utilized in the unending falls an even number of cords while using this technique.

- Begin by completing the first and second steps of Endless Falls. Fill a third cord through the two half-hitches and down through either side of the horizontal cords crossed over the first two. Pulling the crossed strands together will help to tighten up the knot.

- Cross the horizontal cords once again, this time from right to left. Half-hitches should be worked with all four vertical cords, with each cord being brought down on the righthand side of the half-hitch. Make sure to pull the horizontal side cords to tighten up the knot.

- Step 2 is repeated, but this time the vertical cables on the left-hand side of each half-hitch are brought down instead. Continue to repeat these two rows until the braid reaches the desired length, decreasing the length back to two half-hitches after the process.

4.5 HOW TO MAKE MACRAM CRAFTS BETTER WITH BEADS?

Even though macramé is an appealing knotting method when left unadorned, it can be readily decorated with beads and jewels to produce a variety of looks. One of the most popular methods for embellished macramé is the creation of bracelets, which are made by incorporating sparkling beads into a single row of square knots.

Adding Beads to Core Cords

When stringing beads onto core cords, it is more convenient to thread them all simultaneously than adding beads one at a time as you need them.

- Working the initial macramé over single or double core cords, depending on the size of the bead hole, is recommended. After you've added the bead, use a spring clip to attach the cable at the bottom of your board.

- Bring the first bead up to the final knot. Bring the working cords down on each side of the bead and tie a square knot underneath them to secure them. You may use one or more square knots to connect the beads.

- Half-hitches should be worked until the macramé has been twisted around to bring the working cords back out at the sides before attaching a bead to the end of the piece.

Adding Beads to Working Cords

There is just a single strand of cable to pass the beads through when added to the working cords, and the beads may be smaller when added.

- Beads are added as you work. The beads you need should be added to each working string and pushed up to the preceding knot.

- Work the next macramé knot around the core cords in the same manner as you did previously. Continue to add beads to the outer working cords after each knot in the chain.

- The outside working cords of macramé are continued down to the next row of knots on a larger band of the technique. Each of these cords may have a bead sewn onto it to form the beginning of the next row of knots.

- You may attach a bead to the end of each of these strands to make a beautiful border for your project.

Adding Rhinestones

Cup chain, also known as rhinestone or diamantE chain, is a snake-like strip of tiny crystals in settings connected with short bars. It is often used to create exotic costume jewelry since it can mimic more costly diamonds.

- Secure two shorter strands of 1mm cable for the core cords and two longer strands for the working cords with one long strand of 1mm cord each.

- Square knots are used to create a macramé segment. Place the rhinestone cup chain on top of the core cords and secure it with a safety pin.

- Tie the first half of the square knot by passing a length of the left-hand cord through all of the core cords and chain, then over the length of the right-hand cord. Pull the cords up so that the knot is between the first two rhinestones on each side of the knot.

- Finish by working the second part of the square knot, with the right-hand cord passing under and over both core cords and the chain and pulling up so that the knot is also between the first two rhinestones.

- Repetition of steps 2 and 3 will allow you to tie a square knot between each of the rhinestones until you have finished the whole length of the chain.

- Finish with a piece of unadorned square knot macramé to complete the look.

- Cut the rhinestone cup chain using wire cutters, extending and cutting the chain so that the metal lug is level with the next setting on the cup chain.

Selection of Beads and Cords

Adding beads of various shapes and sizes to your macramé project as you go along is permissible, provided that the string can pass through the bead hole. The amount of the beads and string you use will depend on whether you want to make a chunky pattern or a piece of micro macramé, but the methods you employ will be the same regardless of the look you are aiming for.

Simple square knot braids with beads or rhinestone cup chain are used to create these brilliantly colored bracelets that are beautiful and functional. The ingenious design begins with a cord loop, after which the tails are utilized to make a beautiful Chinese button knot for a toggle closure.

4.6 MACRAM FINISHING TECHNIQUES

Knotting methods all include at least one raw end that has to be neatened or covered in some manner before being used to create a piece of jewelry, an accessory, or any other item of clothing. In traditional knotting methods such as whipping or button knots, the raw ends are covered by the knotting cord itself. However, you may also use a variety of findings and fastenings that have been specifically created for this purpose.

Neatening Raw Ends

Since cords and braids tend to splay out at the end, it is necessary to tidy up the end in some manner before inserting it into a clasp or a finding. The method you use to neaten raw ends will depend on the number of strands and kind of material you are working with, and these factors will determine the technique you select:

Melting

When using nylon knotting rope or paracord, neaten the end first by holding it in a flame for a second or two. A home gas lighter will do for a few seconds to melt the end and fuse the raw ends before continuing. Make sure to use caution while melting the ends of your rope with a gaslighter to prevent burning your fingers.

Wrapping

Finish braided or corded ends using strong beading, sewing thread, or fine wire before adding a finding to the braid or cord. The breadth of the rope is very slightly increased as a result of this method.

- Using the thread or wire, carefully wrap it neatly around the cord towards the end, ensuring that the wrapping is even and that the beginning end is trapped below. Don't wrap it too tightly, or it will become too bulky.

- Stitch the tail of the threads beneath the wrapped threads using a sewing needle.
- Trim the tail, and if required, trim across the top of the rope and the bottom.

Whipping

If you want a more beautiful whipped finish, you may use a thicker cable. This method may also construct a loop on a single end of a rope or over a double rope, as described here.

- Making a loop from the thin cord and placing it on the braid or looped braid will give it a finished look. Wrap the working end around the braid from the bottom up and over both loop cords a few times, then cut the working end.
- Continue wrapping the tiny cable in a single layer to achieve a single depth of wrapping. Insert the working end into the loop, keeping the cords clean and tidy throughout the process.
- The thin cord loop's tail should be pulled carefully and then tugged until the loop is buried beneath the whipping.
- Trim both tails to a professional appearance.

Finishing Techniques with End Caps and Cones

There are various shapes and types of cord end, end cap, and cone that may be used to finish raw ends, and some of the many options are discussed in this section.

- Decorative cord ends are tiny metal embellishments that are used to conceal one or more fine raw ends.

- End caps, which may be square, rectangular, or circular, are bigger than cord ends and ideal for thick ropes or braids since they are larger than cord ends. Both sizes are equipped with either a solid ring or a hole through which a fastener may be inserted.

It is critical to ensure that the interior width or dimensions of the finding correspond to the diameter or size of the cable or braid being used.

How to Add End Cone or Cap?

- Fine sewing or beading thread should be used to wrap the end of the braid, making sure that the wrapping is not too deep to be concealed within the end cap; cut the end cap neatly.
- With the end cap closed, spread a little glue over the inner rim with the cocktail stick, putting a drop or two of glue within at the bottom as well. It is important not to get adhesive on the outside of the finding.
- Push the braid or cords into the end cap, ensuring that it is straight and that no raw ends are protruding; you may use a dressmaker's pin to tuck any stray fibers into the cap if they are visible.
- Repeat the process on the other end, and then allow it to dry for 24 hours.

Some end cone or cap types feature a hole rather than a ring at the end of the cone or cap. The braid may be finished with a simple or wrapped loop created with wire or a headpin attached to the braid. Choose a style appropriate for the method, ensuring that all raw ends are covered and that the edge of the end cap or cone fits tightly around the braid or cords.

- Using thread or fine wire, wrap, whip, or tie the end of the braid or bundle of cords, ensuring that the end cap will still fit over the braid or bundle of cords.

- The headpin should be bent over approximately 6mm from the end and inserted beneath the wrapping.

- The headpin should be brought out in the center of one of the braid's ends. Bend the end of the headpin back up over the wrapping, towards where it meets the braid end, using snipe-nose pliers.

- Insert the braid through the hole in the end cap or cone after applying adhesive to the interior of the cap or cone.

- Finish up with a simple loop at the end of the headpin. If the hole is very big, you may use a tiny bead to close the opening before completing the loop.

4.7 MACRAM MATERIALS GUIDE

Before tying your knots, you must first mount all of your supplies on a flat surface. This is where it varies significantly from traditional knitting or crocheting techniques. When doing such crafts, you utilize the yarn as you go rather than starting with a skein. When working with macramé, you must first calculate the quantity of material that will be needed and then mount it.

It becomes more essential to manage your materials. Even modest projects will often require the purchase of many yards or meters of material. It may seem daunting at first, but with a little experience, you will be able to estimate your requirements before starting any job properly. If the design asks for complex knots, the more material you'll need to complete the project.

If your design has a large number of half-and double-half-hitch knots, you'll need to make adjustments to account for the fact that these knots use a significant amount of cord. Although the material amounts for the projects in this book are provided, if you want to experiment with modifications or create your macramé patterns, you'll need to know how to calculate the quantity of material you'll need.

For most projects, you'll need each cable to be at least four to six times the final length of your project. This is a substantial amount of cord or yarn, and dealing with it may sometimes be a headache. To make controlling the yardage simpler, the extra-long ends are carefully picked up using various types of bobbins.

It is possible to conserve materials when knotting sequences do not alter the filler cords, such as making a basic belt out of square knots and twist knots, although this is not always possible. Those fillers should be slightly longer than your final length when the cables are placed on the wall. The length of the knotting cords will be about four times the ultimate length.

A little amount of additional material should be provided for tying off at the end. It is always preferable to have more than you need rather than not enough. If you find yourself with excess materials after completing your project, you may wish to keep a record of them in a notebook for future reference. If you decide to recreate the project again, you may buy a more exact quantity of materials.

Using Bobbins For Thin Cords

When a project necessitates the use of long lengths of cord, bobbins may make them more manageable and prevent them from getting tangled in one another. When working with thick materials, such as yarn, refer to the technique described below instead.

It is possible to wrap the material around a threaded spool and enclose that wrapped length within a bobbin. These bobbins may be found in local bead and craft stores as well as on the internet.

- The excess wire should be wrapped around the core of the bobbin as if you were loading an old-timer.

- Once you've wrapped enough material around the bobbin, shut the bobbin to prevent the string from unraveling.

- They're a lot simpler to deal with when the cables are tied into their bobbins, which makes sense. These bobbins let you unwind your material as and when you need it to be done.

Working With Thick Fibers

Even though most people like plastic bobbins, while working with thick materials such as yarn or leather lace, you'll need a different method of organizing your resources.

- Wrap a piece of yarn or other thick material around your hand to keep it from unraveling.
- Make a loop of cord in a contrasting color and tie it around the loop. When you need more material, just untie, unwrap, and retie the knot.

4.8 JEWELRY MAKING TECHNIQUES

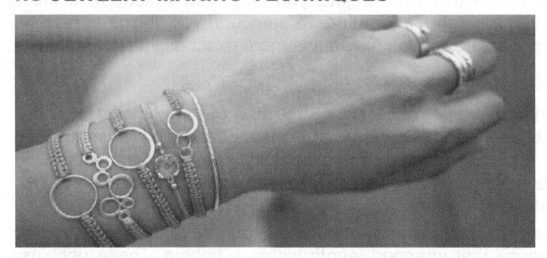

While macramé is at the heart of all of the projects in this book, the jewelry designs require a few other fundamental jewelry-making methods to be completed. If you're a novice, don't be discouraged: everything is laid out for you here, step by step. Round-nose pliers, chain-nose pliers, and wire cutters will all be necessary tools for this project.

Wire Wrapping

Wire wrapping is a secure and long-lasting method of creating connections for attaching chains, charms, beads, or other embellishments. When starting, pick a cheap and smaller wire in gauge than the wire you will be working with later on. Wrap the pliers in a loop and secure them with a knot.

- Wrap a loop around the end of your length of wire using round-nose pliers, approximately 1 inch from the end of the wire.

- Make use of your finger to assist in guiding the tail into position. If the tail is 90 degrees from the body of the wire and the loop that has been created, it is okay to use that length of wire.

- If you wish to connect a length of chain, a jump ring, or another link to the loop, do it immediately before you finish winding it up.

- Remove the pliers from the inside of the loop and place them on the outside of the loop to grip the loop. Grasp the tail of the wire using chain nose pliers and wrap it around the body of the wire, right below the loop, until it is secure.

- Wrap the tail around the wire a total of two or three times. Wire cutters may be used to trim away any surplus. Squeeze the wraps using chain-nose pliers, ensuring the end of the wire isn't sticking out so that it doesn't scratch the person wearing them.

- Add your bead, chain, or finding, and wrap another loop flush against it, just as you did in step 1 to complete the design. Before wrapping the link closed, thread on any chain, jump rings, or other links you want, just as you did in step 2.

Ear Wires Making

Ear wires for earrings are available in several forms, sizes, styles, and metal kinds that may be purchased at a craft store. If you're like me and like to make things from scratch whenever feasible, you may follow these easy steps to create your version. The only other equipment you'll need is a dowel and, perhaps, a metal file or an emery board to finish the job.

- 2" pieces of wire should be cut in half. To create a tiny loop, grab the end of one wire with the round-nose pliers and tighten the loop. Repeat the process with the other wire.

- Take hold of the wire at the loop and gently wrap it around the dowel to give it some dimension.

- This procedure should be repeated with the second wire to verify that the ear wires are the same length.

- Make a slight bend at the top of the ear wire using round-nose pliers to help it fit more comfortably in the ear. With a file or emery board, smooth down any rough edges on the wires that may have formed.

How to Make a Decorative Clasp?

Once again, you may purchase a selection of beautiful clasps for your jewelry creations, or you can follow these easy instructions to create your own with little effort. These clasps may be produced in any size and range of wire gauges and metal kinds to suit your specific needs.

- Begin with a piece of sterling silver 16–18g wire that is about 6cm in length. Place it on a bench block and pound one of the wire ends flat with a jewelry hammer to complete the project.

- Using the round-nose pliers, create a tiny ornamental loop at the end of the wire using the wire cutters. This tiny loop also has a practical purpose in that it provides a smooth end for the hook to slide through to link the necklace to the opposite side's loop.

- Maintaining your hold on the wire with the round-nose pliers, grab it approximately 6mm down from the first tiny loop and wrap it around the thick portion of the pliers in a direction opposite the first loop.

- You've got something to hang your hat on now. Using your fingers and the pliers, make any necessary adjustments to the hook.

- Creating the loop that will link the hook to the remainder of the necklace's chain is now necessary. Start a wire wrap loop approximately 3mm below the bottom of the hook with the round-nose pliers and work your way up.

- Holding the wire tail in your hands, wrap it around the loop you just created with the pliers 2–3 times to make a beautiful coil of wire.

- Trim the end of the piece close to the wrap. Remove any extra wire and use a file to flatten the end if it is very sharp.

Once you've finished the form of the hook and are happy with it, gently hammer the hook's body on the bench block to secure it. This will flatten the hook while also work-hardening the metal, which is essential. It is possible to strengthen the metal, making it stiffer and less prone to lose its form due to the procedure.

5.

MACRAMÉ PROJECT IDEAS FOR BEGINNERS

The Macramé patterns that follow will provide you with a fair example of the variety of things that may be made with knots. There are various methods by which you can find excellent patterns for any number of macramé crafts. In this first section of projects I will show you some very simple ones. To make them, you'll just need to practice what you've learned so far, practicing with the basic knots.

5.1 B. TTERFLY PIN

This pin is quick and simple to make, making it an excellent first-time project. You can make more than one and give them to your family and friends as a gift.

Material

- Glue
- Masking tape
- 3 ft of 1mm hemp
- A jewelry pin
- 3 wooden beads in the size of 14 inches

Directions

1. Make three 12 inch lengths of hemp cord from one piece of hemp cable.
2. Fold one cord in half and tape the folded end to the table, or pin it to your Macramé craft board with a safety pin.
3. Slide a bead onto the cord, bringing it up to within 2 inches of the fold.

4. Bring the other two strands of cord together and slide them beneath the folded strands near the bead to complete the design.

5. Using the double strand of cording, tie a square knot close to the bead, securing it in place.

6. Create another square knot around 12 inches away from the previous knot. The knot should be pushed up to meet the initial knot. The top wings of the butterfly will be formed from this.

7. Attach the last two beads to the cording with your fingers. Create a final square knot about 12 inches from the last bead to complete the design.

8. Continue to pull the knot up until it reaches the last bead, forming the bottom wings of the butterfly.

9. Apply a little glob of glue to the last knot on the string. Allow it to dry completely before using.

10. Cut the double strands close to the last knot in the knotted section. Trim the anchoring cords from the last knot.

11. Remove the masking tape.

12. Fold the cords in half and cut them at the fold.

13. Create the butterfly's antennae by tying a knot in each of the three cords.

14. Trim the ends to within a few inches of the knots.

15. Using hot glue, attach the finished butterfly to the jewelry pin.

5.2 SIMPLE MACRAM KEYCHAIN

It is another newbie project that will help you become more familiar with the macramé technique.

Actually, making macramé keychains is really a great way to experiment and learn by doing. That's why you'll find this item in more than one design proposal! Anyway, feel free to create and find the most appealing knot combination for you.

Material

- 1 keyring
- 6 yards of 1mm hemp
- 3 wooden beads
- Masking tape

Directions

1. Divide the yards of hemp into two halves, each measuring 3 yards.
2. Then, using a half hitch knot, attach them to the metal key chain by threading the folded end of each cord through the keyring and pulling both ends of the cord down through the folded end of the loop.
3. With two cords attached to the keyring, you will now have a total of four functional cords.
4. Attach the keyring to your board with a safety pin.
5. Tie 4 square knots together.
6. Attach the first wooden bead to the two middle cords using the two middle cords as guides.
7. Tie a square knot directly below the bead with your thread.
8. Repeat the process with another bead, creating another square knot directly below the first one.
9. Repeat the process one more time.
10. Make three more knots under the last bead to complete the design.
11. Tie the four cords together in a single large knot.
12. Cut the knot as close as possible.

5.3 A STRIPED CLOVE HITCH KEYCHAIN

A keychain may look extravagant and cluttered—however, it just takes two fundamental knots to get its snazzy custom-colored palette.

1. Start with two 20 or so bits of string (you can generally cut them shorter, so it's smarter to begin long). Circle each through the keyring with a larkspur hitch, making the outside strands somewhat longer than those within.
2. Include vertical clove hitch knots with a couple of different shades of yarn. This video has simple guidelines to kick you off, including how to gauge your wool. We completed two columns each in the initial two colors, and one line in the third color.
3. Make a full square knot in the center.
4. Include another arrangement of vertical clove hitch, turning around what you did on the top.
5. A quick trim of the closures polishes it off.
6. Interlaced and macramé key chains

5. 4 MAKE A FOLDED BRAID KEYCHAIN:

1. This Keychain making is straightforward.
2. Cut three bits of rope somewhat more than twice the length you need for the completed custom keychain.
3. Stack them, even the strands, and wrap one end with a small elastic band a couple of inches from the terms.
4. Do a straightforward mesh. Stop when you are the same distance from the closures as the elastic band is.
5. Circle one end through the keychain. Put the elastic band around the two closures to hold them erect if you'd like.
6. Tie knots in the bargains to wrap it up.

5.5 TASSEL AND MACRAM KEYCHAINS

Supplies:

- 1 Keyring
- 3/16 Natural Cotton Piping Cord
- Beads
- Weaving Floss or Yarn
- Small Rubber Band (KEYCHAIN ONLY)
- Scissors

Steps:

1. For both, you'll start with two 50 or so bits of line. Circle each through the keyring with a larkspur hitch, making the outside strands go around 2/3 the length of the string. (See the free download for step-by-step photographs.)
2. For the keychain, make around five square knots, include the globule, make a half square knot underneath it, and tie the rest in a decoration.
3. For the keychain, create around 16 half square knots and end it off with a ribbon.
4. To give your decoration the extravagant ideal shaft, use your preferred yarn colors.
5. Separate the rope at the closures, trim it up, and you're done!

EXPERT TIP:

To cut the base of the tuft impeccably straight, press it level and wrap it with a bit of tape. Cut the tape down the middle, expel it, and ponder the ideal fringe.

6.1 MACRAM BRACELET WITH BEADS

This beaded bracelet is simple to make, but it is still very elegant to wear when it is completed. The bracelet is a popular choice among teenagers.

Materials:

- 2 yards of 1mm hemp
- A pair of opaque beads in each of the different colors

Directions

1. Cut a length of cord 12 inches in length for the center string.
2. Fold the remaining hemp string in half, starting at one end.
3. Fold the center string in half and insert it between the folds.
4. Tie an overhand knot with the three strings held together, make a circle and pull all the cords through.

5. Make sure you have a loop at the top of the knot when you're finished pulling it tight.

6. Tie a square knot by tugging the left cord in front of the middle string.

7. The right string should be pulled over the left string and then wrapped around the back of the center string to secure it. Pull it through the loop and tighten it.

8. Overturn the square knot by pulling the right string in front of the center string and tightening the knot.

9. Pull the left string around the back of the center string, and then pull the center string around the left string. Pull it through the loop and tighten it.

10. Tie a total of five more knots.

11. Tie the first half of the square knot and then thread a white bead onto the center cord to complete the knot. Complete the knot by tying the second half of the knot.

12. Then, thread a white bead onto each of the outside cords and tie the first half of a square knot around each cord.

13. Thread two white beads onto the center string and tie the second half of the square knot around the center string to secure it.

14. Continue this process for each color of bead in your collection.

15. Make five square knots in a row.

16. Tie all three cords together with an overhand knot.

17. This final overhand knot will be threaded through the loop on the other end of the bracelet to secure the bracelet around your wrist.

18. Cut the cording to the required lengths, which may be 1 inch or longer.

6.2 MACRAM WRAP BRACELET

Wrap bracelets offer a playful and casual design. Four different knottings come together to create one long bracelet that looks like four separate bangles when worn. This type of bracelet also comes together fairly quickly. The finished length of this wrap is 28 ½ inches, and it has a bead button closure.

KNOTS USED:

- Vertical Lark's Head Knot
- Double Half Hitch Knot
- Flat Knot (aka square knot)

Supplies:

- Blue Morning C-Lon Cord, 175 inches, x2
- 1 size 7 mm light blue bead (for the button closure)
- 129 dark blue-gray seed beads
- 11 size 5 mm gray beads
- 52 silver seed beads
- 15 size 3mm light blue bicone beads
- Glue

6.4 M. CRAM DOG COLLAR

This straightforward pattern uses alternating square knots to create a collar with two distinct colors for your dog. The collar is designed to fit a medium-sized dog. Lessen or extend the length of cording used to accommodate a smaller or larger dog, respectively.

Material

- Two 4-yard lengths of hemp in 1mm size, cut into quarters.
- A pair of 4-yard lengths of green hemp, 1mm in dia meter.

Directions

1. Fold one natural cord in half.
2. Using your hands, gather the remaining strands together and tie them around the first in a half knot 3 inches from the

fold.

3. Slip the knot into a ring to keep the strands together and secure them.

4. Organize the cording strands in a clockwise direction from left to right.

5. Tie 12 inches of square knots in alternating directions.

6. Tie an overhand knot in the collar to complete the look.

7. Cut the ends to 1 inch in length and slip the collar off the ring to finish.

6.5 MACRAM PET LEASH

It is easy to work out or create the pet leash, and beginners can quickly get around it. Your animals or pets will love it. This design is very flexible and easy to make; the strap's knots are part of this design's flexibility. This design can look like the pet collar if the same decorative knots are used, but it is NOT the same as the pet collar design.

Tools to be used:

- Swivel Hook
- Glue
- 4mm or 6mm cord material

- Project board and pins
- The knots to be used are:
- Square Knots (SK)
- Overhand Knot
- Buttonhole Clasp
- Vertical Larks Head Knot (Vertical LHK)

CALCULATIONS:

- The length of the material (Leash) after the work is done should be determined by you, and after you and after it has been selected, you should try out this calculation
- Length of the leash (in inches) = WC /3 (in yards)
- The length of the Holding cord also increases by 0.5 yards for every 10 inches; the size of the leash is beginning from 20 inches which are 2 yards long (i.e., 20 inches = 2 yards, 30 inches = 2.5 yards, 40 inches = 3 yards....) till you get to your desired leach's length.
- The total amount of materials need, ed depends on this calculation.

Steps

1. Put the two cords vertically on our board after getting their corresponding midpoints and tightly place them close to one another. The longer WC should be on the left because that is what will be used to tie the LHK on the HC

2. A half of the vertical LHK should be made to move using the WC over or under (as the case may be) the HC to have a counter-clockwise loop. Gradually pulling it left, you should make it go over the WC to get the crossing point. Once the crossing point is reached, tie the other half of the Vertical LHK by passing the WC under or over the HC, while pulling it left, give it under the WC also to make the crossing point.

3. More Vertical LHK should be tied and done from the center in the direction of one end. When the first half of the handle is 6 inches, you should stop.

4. The whole sennit or cords should be rotated and back to the center, leaving the WC on the right. Loos should be made in clockwise directions as tying of Knots is resumed, and once the handle attains a length of 12 inches, you should stop

5. The four segments should be brought together, folding the sennit. Locate the WC in the process. Tie an SK using the 2 WC, and it should be tight. The fillers are going to be the short cords

6. Folding the 2 WC means we should have four wires to work with. The user should use a suitable decorative knot alongside this beautiful design; some of the best knots to use alongside are the Square Knot, the Vertical larks head, and the Half hitch with holding cords. A minimum of six inches of material should be attached to the hook at the end of the pet leach.

7. To attach the hook, two cords should be passed through the loop on the hook, and a tight finishing should be tied with the four ropes. The glue usage comes in here as the four wires are being tightened; the adhesive should be used. When it gets dry, all additional materials should be removed or cut to make the work very neat and beautiful. You may also consider another finishing style that entails moving the ends in the strap's direction and putting it under the back of the knots to be substantial.

6.6 DIY M. CRAM   CAMERA STRAP.

Materials

- · Cord macramé.
- · Clasps swivel.
- · The turns in clothing.
- · Material barrier glue.
- · Scarves.

MAKE TIME:

1 hour (drying time plus glue)

Steps:

1. Cut the macramé cord in 2 lengths, 4 yards each.
2. Fold through cord length so 1 yard is on one side, and 3 yards is on the other side. Attach the midpoints through the flat of one swivel loop, leaving out the long ends of the threads.
3. Push each cord's ends into their own circle and draw the taut around the knot.
4. Continue tying a knot in the square. Take the leftmost cord (should be a long one), pass it over two wires in the middle, and under the most extended (other) cable in the right. So put the right cord under the two parts and the left cord up & over. Push this squeeze—half of the knot in the line.
5. Complete the knot in the square by doing a phase 4 reverse. Cross the right cord over the middle two and below the bottom, then cross the bottom rope under the middle two and over the center. Push taut and end a square knot.
6. Continue to tie square knots until the best length for you is your camera cord.
7. Cut the four cords to their ends. Insert all four cables into another knot that swivels. Place a dollop of glue at the end

of each wire, fold the cords over the knot and keep clothespins in place until the glue dries up.

Replace the clips until the glue is dry, and pop the strap over your frame! I love the macramé cord for a camera strap because it's super lightweight and sturdy, and it's relaxed around your back. Traveling too is brilliant — so beautiful to be able to throw your phone off your shoulder and go. And where are you going on your spring travels? Hoping you'll find somewhere nice to cruise early! Will you on your latest macramé strap to your camera?!

7.

MACRAMÉ PROJECT IDEAS: HOME DECÒR

H ere we go. We wander inside a category very beloved by every aspiring macramé knotter: Home decor.

If you've made it this far, you should already be familiar with the main knots. So there's nothing left for you to do but try your hand at these wonderful projects and turn your living space into a unique place.

7.1 D. eam Catcher in Macrame

This capricious macramé project is perfect for making as a present for someone close to your heart.

Material

- Feathers
- One brass ring with a diameter of 4 inches
- 15 pony beads
- Six yards of any cording in the size of 2mm or smaller

Directions

1. Tie one end of the cord to the ring with a piece of thread.
2. Make a series of loops around the ring, making sure to pull the cording tight after each loop.
3. To begin the next row of the web, wrap the cord over and

down around the previous web row. Continue looping until the opening in the center is the size you desire.

4. While you're working on the dream catcher, you can incorporate the beads into the design in any way you want. Before you add the bead, loop the cording around the bead twice and then push the cording through the bead. The bead will then be held in place within the design's web structure.

5. Once the web design is complete, you can wrap the ring with the cording. A double knot is used to secure one end of the ring to the other.

6. Wrap the cording around the ring's entire circumference, and then glue the ends together to keep them in place.

7. Make a piece of cording between 6 and 8 inches in length. Place the beads wherever you'd like, making sure to tie a double knot after the last bead to secure the design.

8. To secure a feather in place, push it through the beads until it is snugly fit.

9. Double knot the cord to the ring to secure it in place.

10. To hang the finished product, tie a piece of 6-inch cording to the top of the dream catcher and tie it to the ceiling.

7.2 M. CRAM PLANT HOLDER - BOHO

Macramé is a popular method to make your own boho-chic roused plant holders. It's a pattern that has been restored from the 70s, and it's surprisingly better. If you're a plant sweetheart, you'll love how these holders will put your plants in plain view both inside and outside.

Here are the three sorts of fundamental bunches we'll be utilizing in the instructional exercise:

- Square bunch
- Half square bunch or winding bunch
- Circle tie

However, if you'd like more practice with these before you begin, look at this accommodating instructional exercise on essential macramé hitches.

Materials:

- 8 bits of the 15-foot long cotton line (3.1mm thick)
- 2" metal ring
- 2 bits of 5-foot rope

Right now, tell you the best way to make a straightforward macramé plant holder that will help you grandstand your preferred hanging plants and put them in plain view.

Instructions:

1. Accumulate every 8 bits of string, overlay into equal parts, and circle through the ring.
2. Utilizing your 5 foot long bit of string, tie a circle tie directly underneath the ring.
3. Take four strands and tie a square bunch. Rehash multiple

times.

4. Rehash this example with the next gathering of 4 ropes, and rehash for the rest of the lines.

5. Leave a 2 ½ inch hole and tie a half square bunch.

6. Rehash until you've made a 5-inch winding.

7. Rehash this example for the rest of the bunch gatherings.

8. Leave a 6-inch hole and make a hybrid square bunch utilizing the two right lines from your first gathering and the two remaining lines from the nearby gathering.

9. Rehash for the rest of the bunch gatherings.

10. Leave a 6-inch hole and make another hybrid square bunch by substituting the strings from the past advance.

11. Leave a 3 ½ inch hole and tie a circle tie.

12. Trim off the overabundance line to make a tufted finish. Just a pre-craft note; if you first look up those particular knots, your macramé plant hanger DIY project will come together much faster for you. If you ever made friendship bracelets in your teens, they're all knots you'd used!

7.3 MacramE Plant Hanger

Just a pre-craft note; if you first look up those particular knots, your macramé plant hanger DIY project will come together much faster for you. If you ever made friendship bracelets in your teens, they're all knots you'd used!

You will need:

- Macramé flowerpot to make the DIY Macramé plant hanger.

- Paint water.

- Cording of cotton, string, or sturdy cord-like yarn (which we used)

- Scissors are.

- Tape Washi.

Directions.

1. Cut the 2.3-meter long rope into ten lengths. Split them in half and loop through the gap on the bag handle to the folded middle. Take the ends of the line and proceed through the loop you made in this earlier stage. Tight drive. Repeat this until five pieces of rope are tied to the handle of each container.

1. Starting at one end, split two from each other and move the remainder sideways. With those two parts, we will make the first knot. We will use this knot in the tutorial, so keep returning to the following few measures if you get stuck.

Let a right strand bend to cross the correct angle over the left rope.

Take the rope on the left (which is still straight) and thread that you built with the two cords through the gap. Pull both ends of the line away before the knot is shaped and is in the correct position. You want the handle to be about 5 cm forward.

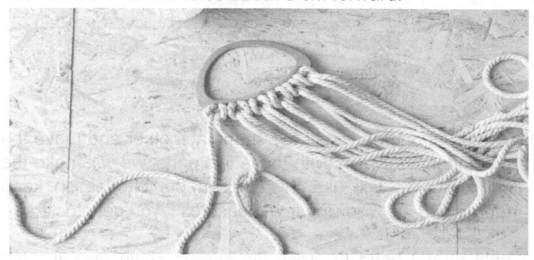

Take the left-hand rope to complete the knot, and this time bring it over the right.

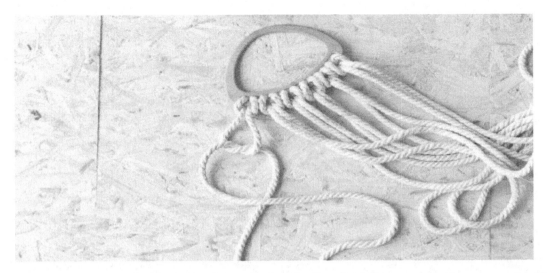

This time the right-hand rope is threaded through the crack. Turn the close tie over again. This is a double half hitch knot now complete.

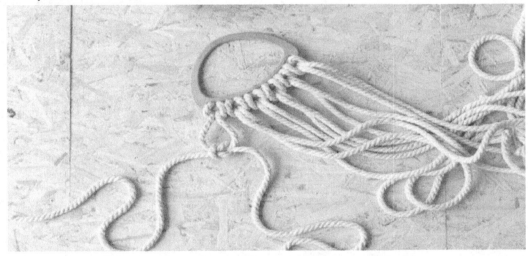

1. Using the remaining ropes on the handle to make four more of those knots in a line. So continue again but skip the first rope this time and the second and third knot. Go on down the line. You'll make four knots this time, and there's no knotting of the first and last rope.

1. Render the third row the same as the first one (thus five loops, without losing any ropes) after you have finished the second row.

2. Repeat steps 2-4 on the second handle until the third row is done. If that's finished, the two handles face each other together with the back ends.

1. Take the two end ropes from both the front and back of the bag and tie these together to start the next. Knot the front and back ties, until you hit the other end. You will then be left in front and back of the last lines. Such ties together.

1. Keep knotting in this style until you are left with around 10 cm of rope on the ropes.

2. Split rope length 4 meters long. Use the same method you used with handles to tie this into the last side knot.

1. Take one front and one back string, and loop the rope around them. Then take two more loops (one from the front and one from the back) and do the same thing. Act before you make it to the top.

1. Draw the rope which hangs down. Connect these threads to stay in place in knots. To strengthen these, you should apply some glue. Combine it to form a fringe.

And you're done with your pack if you want something to dip in a natural burnt red or sage green with a flavored pick.

7.4

MACRAM PLANT HOLDER

This is a perfect project to make extra yarn scraps for friends and family. You can use live plants in your bowl or use a fake one if you're a plant killer like me. Any watering? No watering? That's up my alley — let's start now!

Steps:

1. Cut four different yarn lengths. Mine were about 2 feet long– you want to make sure that your plant holder is enough to

finish! Depending on your planter's size, you may need to make the yarn strands even longer.

2. Fold half the strands of your yarn, then loop the folded end of your chain. Take the loose ends and pull them through the yarn loop you created.

3. Split the yarn into four yarn groupings of two yarn strands each.

4. Measure several centimeters (I just looked at it) and tie each grouping together. Ensure that the knots are about the same length.

5. Document this ad Take the left path of each group and add it to the right way of the next grouping. Keep the knots a little deeper, only an inch or two from the first set of knots. I know it sounds complicated, but it's not, I swear! Take the two external threads and bind them together to create a circular network.

6. Tie one additional round of knots, repeating the process of knotting each group's left strand to the right strand of the next. Bring the ties pretty close to the last round you made– just half or two inches away this time.

7. Tie all the yarn threads a little under the last round of knots you made–around one inch.

8. Given its size, this is a simple project that takes you an hour or two to finish. It gets together quickly, and you will find many ways of adding your style.

9. This is only one of many free macramé patterns, including plant hangers, bookmarks, curtains, and much more.

10. The knots you use to mount this macramé wall include the head knot, the spiral knot, and the square knot.

WHAT YOU WILL NEED TO FINISH:

Cotton Macramé cord (200 feet) and 61 meters (3/4-inch circumference, 24) "wooden dwell (3/4, "24-inch) scissors I've been using cotton clothesline on my macramé string. It looks entirely natural and is relatively cheap.

The wooden dowel must not be exact measurements, and use whatever scale you like in place of the wood dowel as long as all ropes are placed over it. If you want to give it an outdoor experience, you can use a tree branch about the same height.

M. KE A HANGER FOR YOUR WOODEN DOWEL

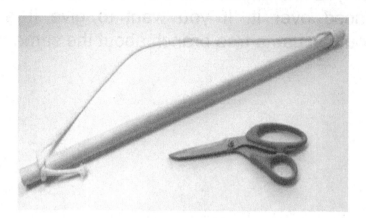

Cut a piece of macramé cord that is three feet (1 meter) and tied to a wooden dowel. Connect the two sides of the wooden dowel to each end of the thread. You will use this to mount your macramé project when it is over. In the beginning, I like to attach it, so I can hang up the macramé project when I tie knots. It is much easier to work this way than to determine it.

Cut your macramé rope into 12 string lengths 15 feet (4.5 meters)

long with a pair of scissors. It might sound like a lot of rope, but knots take up more cord than you expect. If you need it, there's no way to make the rope thicker, so you better cut it than you will.

Fold one of the macramé cores in half on the wooden dowel and use a ladle's head knot to tie it to a wooden dowel.

Join the other cords in the same way

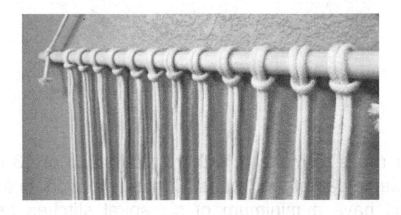

Take the first four strings and make a left-facing spiral stitch (also referred to as a half-knot Lynton) by tying 13 half knots.

Using four ropes to make a further spiral stitch of 13 half knots using the same pair of four ropes. Continue to work in four-chord. You should have a minimum of six spiral stitches before you finish.

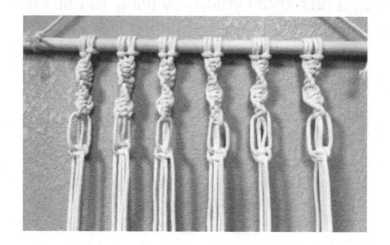

Scale about two inches down from the last knot in a spiral point. This is where your next knot, the square knot, will be found.

Make a right knot profile with the first four strings. Continue to make the correct knots face throughout this row. Do your best to keep them all even horizontally. You're going to end up with six knots together.

The second row of square knots Now is the time to start the square knots to have the "V" shape.

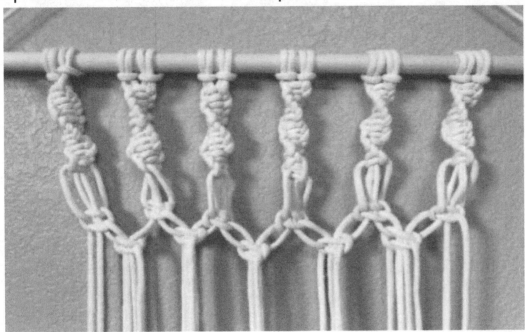

Set open the first two strings and the last two strings. Consider each group of four right-facing square knots. You now have a second line with the first two and last two unknotted cords and five square knots. It doesn't matter how you space them; keep them for each row together.

Keep Decreasing the Square knots A "V" formed from the square knots in the third row, the first four strings, and the last four strings will be left out. You're going to have four knots together. For the fourth row at the top, leave six cords and at the end six cords. You're going to have 3 square ties. In the fifth row, in the beginning, you'll have eight cords and at the end eight cords. Now you're going to have two square ties. Ten cords at the beginning and ten at the end are released for the sixth and final row. It lets you make a last square knot with four strings.

Square Knots Square Making a second "V' in square knots Next time, we'll increase them into a triangle or an upside-down" V.

"For this first segment, bring out the first eight and last eight cords. That will make two square knots.

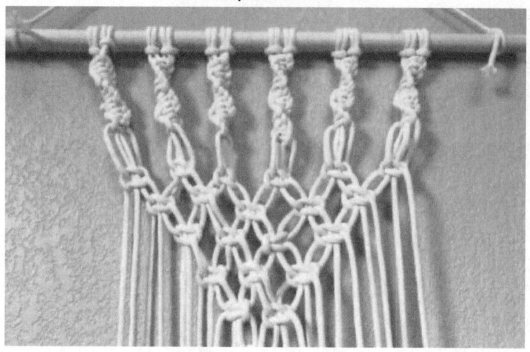

7.5 H. NGING WALL IN MACRAM

- Cut out seventeen white (17) big cords;
- nine (9) red cords;
- get a macramé board
- a pair of scissors
- a wooden pole
- a nail.

NOTE:

The white wires you cut should be very long, enough for the project even when it is folded.

Directions

1. Arrange the red cords on your macramé board. Get a rope out of the seventeen white (17) and tie the line at the two ends of the wooden pole. Entwine every one with the remaining sixteen (16) cords to the pole using the lark's head knotting method.

2. When this is done, get the first four cords from the left-hand side and entwine them using the square knotting method.

3. Take the nearest four wires and make the same pattern with them. Continue with this until the first stage of the work is completed. To go over the second stage, leave the first two cords from the left-hand side and make a square knot with the nearest four wires; make another, and another until you get to the last where two wires will be remaining like it is with the first.

4. Going over to the third stage, take the first four cords from the left-hand side and make the same square knotting pattern with them; continue with this until you get to the last of the third stage.

5. At this point, get one of the red cords, count out the first four cords from the left-hand side, and tie the red rope around the four (4) white ones. Tie it in such a way that it will look aesthetic. You can also make them the same size as your first finger. Just like you tied the first four white cords with a red one, match the last four white wires with a red one too. Do not forget to make them be of the same length to give your work a great look.

6. Going over to the fourth set of the pattern, count out the first four cords (excluding the ones you already tied) from the left-hand side, make a square knot with the wires, make the same knotting method with the rest of the cables to get the fourth set completed.

7. Tie the current first four cords with a red rope you did with the first set. Count out the last four wires and do the same with them.

8. Go over to the next game and square knot the cords like you have been doing. Tie the first four cords and do the same with the last four. Continue with this pattern until you have tied every four sets of white cords using the red ones. Now, there should be one cord that will remain out of the nine cords you cut.

9. Divide the cords into two and neatly tie each cord at the end of the white cord you tied to the pole. Drive the nail through the part of the wall you have chosen for the work and hang the just concluded project. Your macramé wall hanging design is ready!

7.6 CIRCLE MACRAM WALL HANGING

Materials:

- a nail
- two shiny metallic rings (one small ring and a big ring)
- seventeen (17) cords

- a pair of scissors
- and a macramé board.

Directions:

1. You cut out of the seventeen cords, take sixteen (16), and entwine them to the small ring using the lark's head knotting method.

2. Take the first four cords from the left-hand side and make a square knot with the cords. Take the following four cords, do the same with them, and continue with this method until the first stage of this project is completed.

3. Going over to the second stage, leave the first two cords from the rear at the left-hand side, take the last two of the same knot, take the first two cords from the next knot, and make a square knot with the four cords.

4. Take the nearest four cords and continue with this pattern until the second row of the work is completed, leaving the last two cords at the rear, from the right-hand side just like you did with the first two cords.

5. For the third row, take the first four cords from the left-hand side, make the same square knot with the cords and pattern the rest of this row with the same pattern, leaving no cord undone.

6. At this point, cut out another strong rope and tie the top of the small ring to the big ring, leaving the small one inside the other one. The reason for using a stronger cord is to hold the work firmly in place. When you get your work to the level where it touches the big ring, use a backward lark's head knotting method to entwine every one of your cords to the big ring.

7. Carefully and neatly cut the downside of the remaining cords to your taste. Untie the strong cord you used to tie the two rings and use the only cord remaining out of the seventeen cord you cut earlier to tie the two rings. Do make

sure the tying is carefully and neatly done. Tie it to have a space you will use to hang it.

8. Drive the nail through the part of the wall you have chosen for the work and hang your newly-made project. Your macramé circle wall hanging design is here!

7.7 BOHO MACRAM WALL HANGING

Materials:

- about thirty (30) big and long cords
- a wooden pole
- a pair of scissors
- a nail
- a macramé board.

Directions:

1. Entwine every one of the cords to the wooden pole using the lark's head knotting method.

2. Take the first four cords from the rear at the left-hand side, and make a spiral knot with them. To make this spiral knotting pattern, pick out the first four cords and take the first from the left, over the two at the middle; take the one at the right over the left one, taking the left one into space in-between the left cord itself and the two at the center; pull the two cords to tighten the knot. Take the one at the left over the two in the middle, take the right cord over the left one, take the left cord into space in-between the ones at the center, and pull the two cords. Make four spiral knots for each set.

3. As you do this, you will notice that the knots you are making will be going in a spiral form. Make a spiral knotting pattern with the rest of the cords.

4. At this point, take one of the cords you are yet to use and place it horizontally over the current line of your cords and entwine every single cord using a backward lark's head knot. Take the first four cords from the left-hand side and continue with the square half hitch knots you made earlier.

5. This time, make eight square half hitch knots with each set (four cords). Get another unused cord and place it horizontally over the current line of your cords. Entwine the cords to the horizontally placed one just like the first horizontal one.

6. At this point, pick the first four cords and make a square knotting pattern with them. Pick another four and repeat the pattern until you get every one of the cords to this stage.

7. For the next level, leave the first two cords, pick the nearest four cords after the two and make a square knot with the cords. Carry on with this pattern until you are done with that stage; two cords will remain at the rear from the right-hand side.

8. For the next stage, leave the first four cords and continue with the pattern until you get to the last cords, leaving four cords from the rear at the other side.

9. For the next stage, leave the first six cords and carry on like you have been doing, leaving the same number of cords unattended too. You have to do this until you get to the middle; make the last square knot there since there is no other cord to work the square knot on. Dress the down part of the cords to your taste, make sure the cords are in order, and dress the two ends of the two cords you placed horizontally just above.

10. Get the remaining two cords and tie one of them to the two ends of the pole. Divide the remaining cord into two and make tassels out of them. Tie the cords you will use to hang the tassels to the pole, and attach one tassel at each end of the cord.

11. Drive a nail through the part of the wall you have chosen for the project and hang your work. Your macramé Boho wall

hanging design is ready to grace your home!

7.8 S.mple Macrame Wall Art

Adding a bit of Macramé to your walls is always fun because it livens up the space without making it cramped—or too overwhelming for your taste. It also looks beautiful without being too complicated to make. You can check it out below!

Materials:

- Large wooden beads
- Acrylic paint
- Painter's tape
- Paintbrush
- Wooden dowel
- 70 yards rope

Directions:

1. Attach the dowel to a wall. It's best to use removable hooks only, so you won't have to drill anymore.

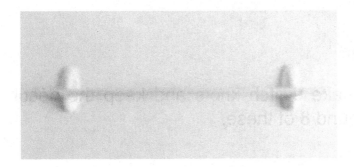

1. Cut the rope into 14 x 4 pieces and 2 x 5 pieces. Use 5-yard parts to bookend the dowel with. Continue doing this with the rest of the rope.
2. Then, start making double half-hitch knots and continue all the way through, like what's shown below.

1. Once you get to the end of the dowel, tie the knots diagonally so that they wouldn't fall or unravel in any way. You can also add the wooden beads any way you want, so you'd get the kind of décor that you need. Make sure to tie the knots after doing so.

1. Use four ropes to make switch knots and keep the décor more secure. Tie around 8 of these.

1. Add a double half hitch and then tie them diagonally once again.

1. Add more beads and then trim the ends of the rope.

1. Once you have trimmed the rope, go ahead and add some paint to it. Summery or neon colors would be right.

1. That's it! You now have your own Macramé Wall Art!

Plant hangers are lovely because they give your house or garden the feel of airy, natural space. This one is perfect for condominiums or small apartments—and those with minimalist, modern themes!

Materials:

- ¤ Plant Pot
- ¤ 50 ft. Par cord (Parachute Cord)
- ¤ 16 to 20 mm wooden beads

Directions:

1. First, fold in half four strands of the wire and then loop so you can form a knot.

to string two wires through one of the wooden beads you have on hand. String some more beads—at least four on each set of 2 grouped wires.

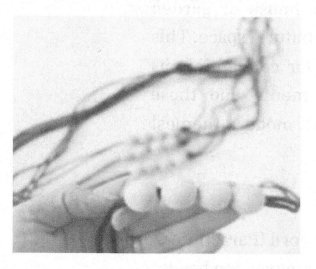

3. Then, measure every 27.5 inches, tie a knot at that point, and repeat this process for every set of cords.

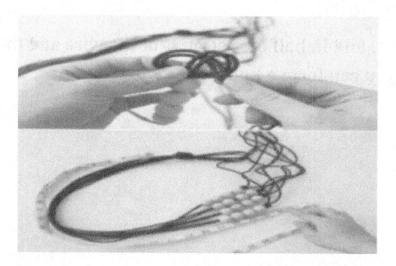

4. Look at the left set of the cord and tie it to the correct string. Repeat on the four games so that you can make at least 3" from the knot you have secured.

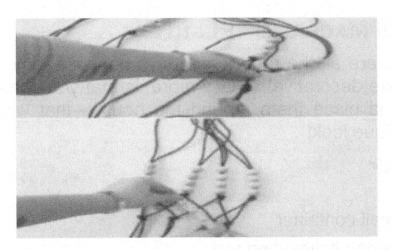

5. Tie another four knots from the knot that you have made. Make them at least 4.5" each.

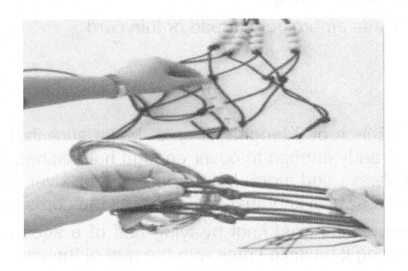

6. Group all of the cords and tie a knot to finish the planter. You'll get something like the one shown below—and you could add your very own planter to it!

7.10 M.ni Macrame Planters

Succulents are all the rage these days because they are just so cute and are decorative! What's more, is that you can make a lot of them and place them around the house—that will give your place a unique look!

Materials:

- Small container
- Garden soil/potting mix
- Succulents/miniature plants
- ¼ inch jump ring
- 8 yards embroidery thread or thin cord

Steps:

1. Cut 36-inch of 8 lengths of cord. Make sure that 18 inches are already enough to cover enough half-hitches. If not, you can always add more. Let the thread loop over the ring and then tie a wrap knot that could hold all the cords together.
2. Create a half-twist knot by tying half of a square knot and repeating it multiple times with the rest of the cord.
3. Drop a quarter inch of the cord down and repeat the step twice.
4. Arrange your planter and place it on the hanger that you have made.
5. Nail to the wall, and enjoy seeing your mini-planter!

7.11 H. NGING MACRAMÉ VASE

To add a delicate, elegant touch to your house, you could create a Macramé Vase. With this one, you'll have to make use of basket stitches/knots—which you'll learn about below. It's also perfect for those who love flowers—and want to add a touch of nature at home!

Materials:

- Masking tape
- Tape measure or ruler
- 30 meters thick nylon cord
- Small round vase (with around 20 cm diameter)

Directions:

1. Cut eight cords measuring 3.5 yards or 3.2 meters each and set aside one of them. Cut a cord that measures 31.5 inches and set it aside, as well. Then, cut one cord that measures 55 inches.

1. Now, group eight lengths of cord together—the ones you didn't set aside, of course, and mark the center with a piece of tape.

2. Wrap the cords by holding them down together and take around 80 cm of it to make a tail—like what you see below.

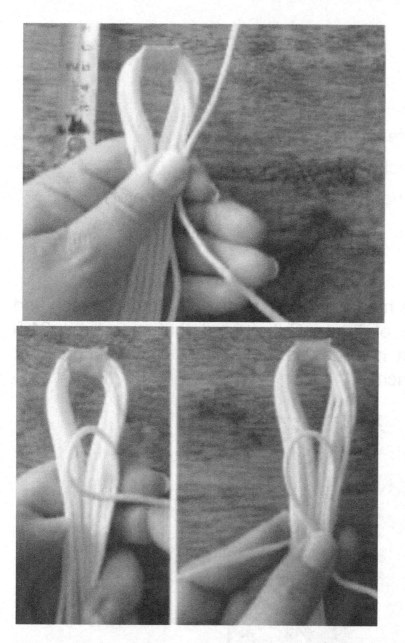

1. Do it 13 more times through the loop and go and pull the tail down so the circuit could soften up. Stop letting the cords overlap by pulling them whenever necessary and then cut

both ends so they would not be seen anymore.

2. Divide the cords into groups of four and secure the ends with tape.

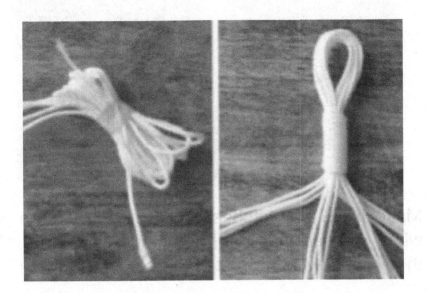

1. Get the group of cords that you have not used yet, and make sure to measure 11.5 inches from the beginning—or on top. Do the overhand knot and get the cable on the left-hand side. Fold it over two cords and let it go under the wire on the right-hand side.

2. Fold the fourth cord and let it pass under the leftmost cord, then up the loop of the first cord. Make sure to push it under the large knot to be substantial.

1. Make more half-hitches until you form more twists. Stop when you see that you have made around 12 of them, and then repeat with the rest of the cords.

1. Now, it's time to make the basket for the vase. What you have to do here is measure 9 centimeters from your group of cords. Tie an overhand knot and make sure to mark with tape.

1. Let the two cord groups come together by laying them side by side.

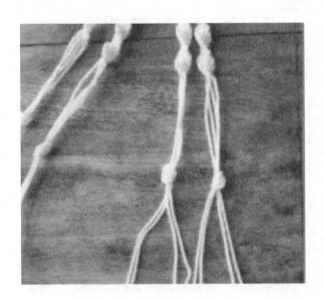

1. Tie the cords down but make sure to keep them flat. Make sure that the knots won't overlap, or else you'd have a messy project—which isn't what you'd want to happen. Use two cords from the left as a starting point, and then bring the two wires on the right over the top of the loop. Loop them together under the bottom ropes and then work them back up once more.

2. Now, find your original loop and thread the same cords

behind them. Then, let them pass through the left-hand cords by using the loop once more.

1. Let the knot move once you already have it in position. It should be around 3 inches or 7.5 cm from the overhand knots. After doing so, ensure that you flatten the cords and let them sit next to each other until you have a firm knot on top. Keep dividing and letting ropes come together.

1. Next, get the cord on the left-hand side and let it go over the 2nd and 3rd cords before folding the fourth one under the first two cords. You'd then see a square knot forming between the 2nd and 3rd cords. You should then repeat the process on the right-hand side. Open the wire on the right side and let it go under the left-hand rope. Repeat this process thrice, then join the four-square knots you have made by laying them out on a table.

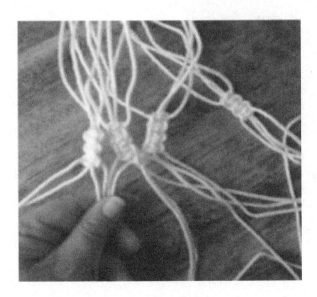

1. You'll then see that the cords have come together at the base. You have to start wrapping the bottom by wrapping a

1.4-meter cord and cover around 18 times.

1. To finish, just cut the cords the way you want. It's okay if they're not of the same length so that there'd be variety—and they'd look prettier on your wall. Make sure to tie overhand knots at the end of each of them before placing the vase inside.

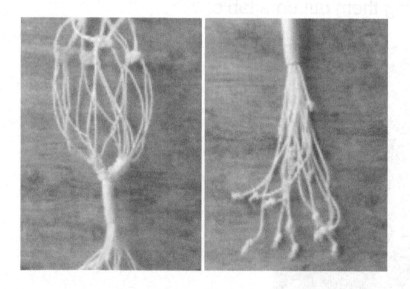

Enjoy your new hanging vase!

7.12 L.VING ROOM MACRAME CURTAIN

Macramé Curtains give your house the feel of that beach house look. You don't even have to add any trinkets or shells—but you can, if you want to. Anyway, here's a high Macramé Curtain that you can make!

Materials:

- Laundry rope (or any rope/cord you want)
- Curtain rod
- Pins
- Lighter
- Tape

Steps:

1. Tie four strands together and secure the top knots with pins so they can hold the structure down.

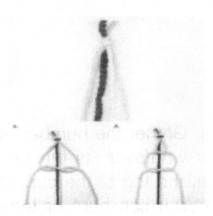

1. Take the strand on the outer right part and cross over to the left side by passing through the middle. Tightly pull the strings together and reverse what you have done earlier.

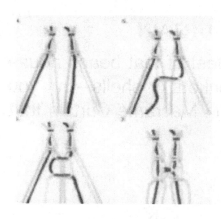

1. Repeat crossing the thread over four more times for the yarn you now have in front of you. Take the strand on the outer left and let it pass through the middle, and then take the right and let it cross over the left side. Repeat as needed, then divide the group of strands to the left and the right. Repeat until you reach the number of rows you want.

1. You can now apply this to the ropes. Gather the number of lines you want—10 to 14 is okay, or whatever fits the rod, with proper spacing. Start knotting at the top of the curtain until you reach your desired length. You can burn or tape the ends to prevent them from unraveling.
2. Braid the ropes together to give them that dreamy, beachside effect, just like what you see below.
3. That's it; you can now use your new curtain!

7.13 C. ALLENGING MACRAMÉ CURTAIN

Supplies required:

- 389 feet of 3/16″ cotton rope
- covering or painter's tape
- scissors
- arrangement

Directions:

Cut 32 bits of rope, each estimating 12 feet. Fold a little bit of tape over the two parts of the line bargains to forestall fraying. Integrate bits of string (as appeared in photograph beneath), with the bunch around 10 crawls from the rope closes.

MACRAMÉ TABLE LINEN

Do this for all the bits of rope so that you will wind up with 16 tied pieces. Lay them equitably on a level surface and tape the closures down to keep consistent.

MACRAMÉ TABLECLOTH

stage 1 – half jewel

Make a Square Knot by utilizing the initial four individual lines on the left to start your structure. Proceed until you have a range of 8 Square Knots.

MACRAMÉ TABLE LINEN

Starting with the third line from the left, make a column of 7 rotating square bunches.

MACRAMÉ TABLECLOTH

You have now completed the initial two columns. Adhere to the guidelines underneath for lines 3 through 8.

- push 3: beginning with fifth individual line from the left – 6K (6 Square Knots)

- push 4: beginning with seventh individual line from the left – 5K
- push 5: beginning with ninth personal track from the left – 4K
- drive 6: beginning with eleventh particular line from the left – 3K
- drive 7: beginning with thirteenth personal line from the left – 2K
- drive 8: start with fifteenth own line from the left – 1K

MACRAME TABLECLOTH

stage 2 – little side jewels

You have now finished the main half precious stone plan. Before proceeding with an inside precious stone, you must add two little jewel shapes to the sides (as demonstrated as follows).

MACRAME TABLECLOTH

For the little jewel on the right side, beginning with the fifth individual line from the right, make a Square Knot. Underneath that tie, starting with the third particular string from the right, make two Square Knots. Once more, underneath those two bunches, beginning with the fifth line from the right, make the last Square Knot. You have now made a small jewel plan. Rehash this technique for the left side.

MACRAME TABLE LINEN

stage 3 – full precious stone

The following step is to make a complete costly stone structure.

MACRAME TABLECLOTH

This precious stone comprises 15 lines. Adhere to the guidelines beneath.

MACRAME TABLE LINEN

- push 1: beginning with fifteenth individual line from the left – make one Square Knot (You can see that this bunch is straightforwardly underneath the keep going bunch on the past half precious stone structure.
- push 2: beginning with thirteenth individual string from the left – 2K
- push 3: start with eleventh own string from the left – 3K
- shift 4: begin with ninth own line from the left – 4K
- drive 5: begin with seventh individual string from the left – 5K
- push 6: beginning with fifth own string from the left – 6K
- push 7: begin with third own string from the left – 7K
- drive 8: beginning with first own line from the left – 8K
- shift 9: begin with third personal line from the left – 7K
- disc 10: beginning with fifth particular line from the left – 6K
- drive 11: beginning with seventh own line from the left – 5K
- drive 12: start with ninth own path from the left – 4K
- disc 13: beginning with eleventh individual line from the left – 3K
- push 14: begin with thirteenth personal rope from the left – 2K
- force 15: start with fifteenth particular rope from the left – make one Square Knot

When this precious stone is finished, include an additional Square Knot just underneath the inside bunch in push 15.

TABLECLOTH

Stage 4 – little side jewels

Follow stage 2 to include two all the littler jewels on the sides.

TABLECLOTH

Stage 5 – focus of sprinter

About 2″ down from the base of the full jewel, make a line of Square Knots. (Beginning with the first individual line on the left, make 8 Square Knots.

MACRAME

Avoid down about 4″ from the last column of Square Knots. Beginning with the seventh individual line from the left, make a Square Knot – avoid four strings – make a Square Knot – skirt four ropes – make a Square Knot – skirt the last six lines.

TABLECLOTH

About 4″ down from the last line, make a column of Square Knots. (Beginning with the first individual line on the left, make 8 Square Knots.

MACRAME TABLECLOTH

Stage 6 – wrapping up

To finish the sprinter, you will mostly be re-making the example in the principal segment of the sprinter (before the inside part). Track with these directions to do this:

The following errand is to buy and make two little jewels as an afterthought. Skirt down about 2″ from the last column and adhere to guidelines in stage 2 to make the two small precious stones.

Presently you will make another full jewel shape, with your first bunch (or top of the precious stone) falling in the focal point of the highest point of the two little jewels. Adhere to the directions in stage 3 to make this entire jewel structure.

By and by, make two precious little stones as an afterthought. Adhere to guidelines in stage 2 to make the two small precious stones.

At last, you will make a half precious stone structure:

- push 1: beginning with fifteenth individual line from the left – make one Square Knot

- shift 2: start with thirteenth own string from the left – 2K

- drive 3: begin with eleventh personal line from the left – 3K

- prompt 4: beginning with ninth individual track from the left – 4K

- push 5: start with seventh own line from the left – 5K

- push 6: beginning with fifth personal line from the left – 6K

- drive 7: beginning with third own line from the left – 7K

- drive 8: start with first own line from the left – 8K

Straightforwardly underneath your last column of Square Knots, beginning with the initial two ropes on the left, tie a customary bunch. Keep tying ties until you have 16 secure bunches.

5.6 DIY M. craME FEATHERS:

Delightful, wispy macramé feathers have been stopping up my online life takes care lately – however, I'm not frantic about it. They're unimaginably lovely and I've certainly gotten myself bookmarking them to buy later, to hang in the children's room. I was likewise curious to know how they were made. How in the world do you accomplish that impeccably delicate fringe?! And it includes a feline brush. That's all anyone needs to know. Indeed, however, the conceivable outcomes are unfathomable here, and I can hardly wait to mess with this method more. Be that as it may. Meanwhile, I trust I'll motivate you to make these at home.

You'll Need:

- 5mm single wind cotton string
- Texture stiffener
- Sharp texture shears
- Feline brush
- Ruler

For a medium measured plume, cut:

- 1 32" strand for the spine
- 10-12 14" strands for the top
- 8-10 12" strands for the center
- 6-8 10" strands for the base

Steps:

1. Overlap the 32" strand into equal parts. Take one of the 14" strands, overlap it down the middle, and fold it under the spine.
2. Take another 14" strand, crease it down the middle and

supplement it into the circle of the top-level strand. Pull it through and lay it horizontally on the restricting strand.

3. Presently pull the base strands all the path through the top circle. This is your knot!

4. Pull the two sides firmly. On the following line, you'll interchange the beginning side. So, if you laid the even strand from left to right the first time, you'll put the level strand from options right to left straightaway.

5. Lay the first collapsed strand under the spine, string another collapsed strand into its circle. Pull the lower strands through the top loop. Also, fix.

6. Continue onward and work gradually down in size.

7. Make sure to push the strands up to fix - snatch the base of the center (spine) strand with one hand and with another, push the strands up. When you're set, drag the fringe downwards to meet the base of the center strand.

8. At that point, give it a rough trim. This helps direct the shape and assists with brushing the strands out. The shorter the strands, the simpler, to be completely honest. It likewise helps to have a sharp pair of texture shears!

9. After a rough trim, place the quill on a stable surface as you'll be using a feline brush to brush out the cording. The brush will harm any fragile or wood surface, so I recommend using a self-mending cutting mat or even a smoothed-out cardboard box.

10. Work your way down. At the point when you're at the base, hold the bottom of the spine while brushing - you don't need the brush to yank any strands off!

11. Next, you'll need to harden the quill. The cording is delicate to such an extent that it'll merely fall if you get it and attempt to hang it. Give it a splash or two, and allow to pursue at least a few hours.

12. When your plume has hardened up a bit, you would now be able to return and give it a last trim. This, I would state, is the most challenging part. Relax. It's smarter to trim just a

little more! What's more, you may need to modify your trim contingent upon how regularly you're moving the piece. When you're ended cutting, you can even give it another wanderer of texture stiffener for good measure. And afterward, you'll be ready to hang your piece!

6.

MORE MACRAMÉ PROJECT IDEAS: JEWELERY

In this section I will show you how you can make original accessories, even with beginner skills! You got it right, from today you can wear your creations and indulge yourself in every possible way to express your creative personality. Below are some project ideas from which you can start.

CONCLUSION

K notting, also known as macramé, is one of many crafts being resurrected by people who enjoy working with their hands. It is being changed from a relic of the 1970s into a hot, trending art form, much like intricate surface designs, knitting and needlework are experiencing a resurgence in popularity these days.

It is a versatile form of fiber art that can create items ranging from wall art and plant hangers to jewelry, purses, and even garments. It can be made out of simple materials such as cotton raffia, jute, synthetic fibers, or yarn, and it can be as simple or as complex as the maker desires. The addition of embellishments such as crystal or wooden beads and colored threads can expand the range of possible design options. Macramé is a type of textile created through knotting techniques rather than weaving or knitting methods. The main knots used in macramé are the square knot and different forms of hitch knots, blended half hitches. It has been used to cover everything from knife handlebars to containers to ship components for hundreds of years by sailors, particularly in intricate or decorative knotting forms. Cavandoli macramé is used to create geometric and free patterns, such as those found in weaving. The double half-hitch knot is used extensively in this style. When working the left and right halves of a balanced piece, it is sometimes necessary to use reverse half hitches to keep the piece balanced. Belts made of leather or fabric are another accessory that is frequently made using macramé techniques. This method is used to make the vast majority of friendship bracelets exchanged among schoolchildren and teenagers. Additionally, vendors may sell macramé jewelry or decorations at theme parks, malls, seasonal fairs, and other public venues. It is common for macramé to be initiated on a wooden frame dowel for larger decorative items such as wall art or heavy curtains, which allows for the spread of many dozens of cords that are easy to control. Push-pin boards designed specifically for macramé designs are readily accessible for smaller projects, though a simple corkboard will suffice for most purposes. Many craft shops carry complete beginner kits, work boards, beadwork, and equipment at various price points to suit the needs of both the casual enthusiast and the aspirational crafter.

Made in the USA
Coppell, TX
18 November 2024

40481985R00098